THE THREE LIVES OF
DYLAN THOMAS

THE THREE LIVES OF DYLAN THOMAS

Hilly Janes

Parthian, Cardigan SA43 1ED
www.parthianbooks.com
First published in 2014
This edition 2018
Copyright © Hilly Janes 2014
ISBN 9781912109814
Cover design by Robert Harries
Typeset by Elaine Sharples
Printed and bound in Bulgaria by pulsioprint.co.uk
Published with the financial support of the Welsh Books Council,
Etxepare Institutoa Translation Grant,
and OMI Writers Translator Lab Award
British Library Cataloguing in Publication Data
A cataloguing record for this book is available from the British Library.

To Andrew, Suzi, Ali and Ross

Hannah Ellis, Dylan's granddaughter, at the launch of the
Dylan Thomas 100 centenary programme

WHAT A DIFFERENCE A YEAR MAKES

What a difference a year makes. The first edition of this book was finished just as Dylan Thomas 100, the centenary celebration of the poet's birth, got underway in 2014. By the end of the year, he had indeed been trumpeted from fish to jumping hill, to paraphrase a line from 'Prologue' – in theatres, cinemas, galleries, concert and lecture halls, schools, bookshops, newsrooms, heritage centres and of course, pubs. And not just in Wales – hundreds of events took place around the UK and as far afield as Argentina, India, Canada, Australia and the USA.

The prolific letter-writer even got his own First Day Cover with a special stamp from the Royal Mail, and digital platforms invented long after this brilliant broadcaster died spread the word to younger generations via new apps, Facebook and Twitter. 'Do not go gentle…', the opening words of what has always been one of his best-loved poems, have become an internet meme and a battle cry for protest movements around the world.

If Dylan Thomas took centre stage again, actors and musicians who retold his story basked in his reflected glory. A host of stellar performers took part in a 'Dylathon', a marathon thirty-six hour reading of his work in Swansea. *Under Milk Wood* got a new touring production, a film version in Welsh and a new BBC Wales TV film – part of a dedicated Dylan season. The cast lists were a roll call of top Welsh theatrical talent.

Many of them also turned out for a gala concert at London's Southbank Centre, the culmination of Dylan Thomas in Fitzrovia, a weekend jamboree on his old BBC stamping ground. The following year, Tom Hollander won the Royal Television Society's Best Actor award for his depiction of Dylan in *A Poet in New York*. *Set Fire To The Stars,* a black and white film about Dylan and his US promoter made on a shoestring in ten days in Swansea and Cardiff also won three prizes, including for Original Music Score for the jazzy soundtrack by Gruff Rhys.

There were exciting developments too, like the discovery of a long-lost fifth notebook in which he wrote his poetry in a Tesco bag stuffed in a kitchen drawer, acquired by Swansea University at Sotheby's for £104,000. The BBC created an invaluable Dylan Thomas archive of clips on its website. The poet's granddaughter, Hannah Ellis, launched a new portal, discoverdylanthomas.com. Funded by the literary trust founded after his death in 1953 (which no doubt reaped centenary rewards), it showcases events and news, and gives access to the many global online resources related to her grandfather.

The Welsh government, the penny having finally dropped that they were onto a good thing, announced an annual International Dylan Thomas Day, although mysteriously not on 27 October, his birthday, but on 14 May, the date that *Under Milk Wood* was first performed in New York. It reported a pleasing return on its £1m plus investment in DT100, which helped to fuel an increase to £360m in tourism revenue in 2014 in Swansea Bay alone, with spending in Wales overall by domestic visitors and trips from international visitors increasing by 10 per cent. It came as no surprise that Cardiff-born Roald Dahl got the 100 treatment two years later.

But the centenary would have not been true to the man without a little controversy. An unsavoury dispute over ownership of the rights to some early photographs of Dylan led to litigation in Ireland. Despite the re-publication of much of his work, and a completely revised edition of the *Collected Poems*, there were accusations of dumbing down from academic quarters. 'Brand

Dylan', it was argued, was being used as a promotional tool for other interests, with too much frothy focus on the life and not enough scholarly exploration of the work.

More fur flew over a proposed wind turbine that would spoil the view across the estuary from Dylan's home at the Boat House and his writing shed in Laugharne. Dylan fans demanded a judicial review of the proposal, and won. Sadly the Dylan effect did not spread as far as the Ceri Richards Gallery at Swansea University. Dedicated to another hugely talented and internationally acclaimed artist born in the town, who produced many paintings and prints inspired by his poetry, it closed in December 2017.

The multiple strands and huge reach of the 100th birthday celebrations reminded me of something my father, the artist Alfred Janes, wrote about his friend, that he: 'comprised multiple, diverse personalities – each one a stranger to the rest. He could be punctilious, outrageous, comic, tragic, or just totally unexceptional. The intelligentsia, the bartenders and even the herons could easily take him as one of themselves'. Whether your nose is in a book, a pint glass or savouring the whiff of salt on a stiff Welsh breeze, Dylan Thomas will be a willing companion.

Where does it all leave the man and his work? A little less the drunken Welshman and far more the revered writer, certainly. But there is more to it than than that. Dylan left school at 16 having passed only one public exam – in English. He failed to hold down a regular job, always struggled to earn a living, and was written off as a drunk by many. But through his talent, scholarship, wit and charm he taught many people who might not otherwise have done so to 'love the words', in both written and spoken English, demonstrating the power of the arts to transform our lives. Not bad for a no-good Swansea boyo.

Hilly Janes
London, 2018

CONTENTS

Part Three: Did Not Go Gentle

'*Dylan Thomas was a most lovable fellow and I shall always count the hours spent in his company as the most precious gift from the gods, when one's sense of being alive was increased tenfold. I am profoundly grateful of having been one of his countless friends.*'
– Alfred Janes

'*Love the words.*'
– Dylan Thomas

INTRODUCTION

Dylan Thomas had many faces, but few people knew them as well as the artist Alfred Janes, my late father – Fred as he was known to family and friends. Over the course of the poet's short thirty-nine-year life, Fred painted his portrait three times – hence the title of this book. The first was made in 1934 when Dylan's first book of poems was about to be published, the second nearly twenty years later in 1953, the year that he died in a New York hospital. Ten years later Fred made a posthumous drawing of his friend to coincide with the first full-length biography of the poet, whose reputation was by then legendary, and not always for the right reasons.

With these three portraits as its anchor, *The Three Lives of Dylan Thomas* tells the story of three very different stages of Dylan's life and afterlife, from the 1930s, when he was a highly promising teenage poet, to his rock star-like status as a performer in the 1950s. Finally, and unlike most other accounts of his life, it reveals what he left behind – not just his tremendous literary output and its financial rewards, but the impact of his early death on his family and friends. Sixty-five years after Dylan Thomas died, his ghost is still a powerful presence in the lives of many people. He was a drunken, hell-raising, womanising sponger. The description has been repeated so many times by countless associates and acquaintances that he has become a mythical creature. Readers who are looking to put flesh on the bones of that Dylan Thomas may be disappointed by this book. It aims to put forward a different point of view through the words and images of the

1

people who were closest to him – the writers, artists and musicians that he grew up with in his hometown, Swansea, and his close relatives. And of course of Dylan himself, not only in his poetry, but his short stories, plays, broadcasts and letters. No one would deny that Dylan drank too much and that he could be a troublesome drunk, or that he slept with a lot of women and was a charming flirt. But Dylan was rarely the seducer, as even his wife Caitlin pointed out. He relied heavily on the generosity of these close friends, but they understood the difficulties of making a living from the arts, especially in an industrial town in south Wales ruined first by the Great Depression and then by Hitler's bombs. Dylan rarely, if ever, took advantage of people who were as badly or worse off than he was. Fred recognised the ugly side of Dylan Thomas of course; they were close friends for more than twenty years. But he also saw many other faces of the poet at close quarters. There was the sixteen-year-old dropout with a masterly knowledge of English literature thanks to his father, an English teacher who taught both boys and whose study at home was lined with books that Dylan devoured. At the house of a mutual school friend, Daniel Jones, a brilliant student of English and music, Fred discovered Dylan's gift for wordplay, sense of rhythm and appetite for making mischief, as well as a flair for acting and mimicry – the qualities that made him such sought-after company in the pubs and clubs of London's Fitzrovia. When Fred went to study portraiture at the Royal Academy Schools in London and Dylan later moved in with him, they shared digs with Mervyn Levy, another artist from Swansea who first met Dylan at junior school. Fred witnessed their shared love of creating hilarious fantasy characters and surreal stories that could go on for days. He also appreciated Dylan's compassion for down-and-outs and the victims of the burgeoning fascist movement in 1930s London. And he saw what many people missed – how tremendously hard

Dylan worked, writing and rewriting with enormous dedication and craftsmanship.

At Dylan's home in Cwmdonkin Drive in Swansea's genteel suburbs, Fred discovered the power the young poet could wield over an audience when he read his work aloud, and he listened, spellbound. Sometimes they would be in the company of another young Swansea poet whom Dylan had got to know, Vernon Watkins. These friends and their wider circle in Swansea discussed their ideas, stimulating and nurturing each other in a town that was more interested in chapel and commerce than paintings and poems. They were all successful on their own terms, producing poetry, stories, plays, radio and TV broadcasts, orchestral music, paintings and books on art that were underpinned by technical mastery and a fiercely independent mindset. Their achievements were recognised far beyond Wales, and while none of them became as famous as Dylan Thomas, they became painfully aware of how his rackety celebrity lifestyle ruined his health, wrecked his family life and contributed to his early death.

Close to Dylan too, of course, were his family. Most biographies of Dylan have been written by men of an older generation, but as a wife and mother I hope to bring fresh perspective to the story of his personal life. The self-styled Rimbaud of Cwmdonkin Drive never lived very far away from the conventional comforts of his parents and was particularly close to his mother. Florence Thomas has usually been disparaged as a mere housewife and molly-coddler. She certainly turned a blind eye to the less attractive aspects of her son's character, but in doing so Florence offered a safe haven not just to her son but to his children, when his tempestuous marriage to Caitlin hit stormy waters. After Dylan's death Florence was often a guest at our home on the Gower peninsula and I hope to shed new light on the important role she played in his life, right until the end, based on hitherto unpublished letters and accounts of her visits.

3

Dylan left three young children when he died. It fell to his only daughter, Aeronwy, to pick up the mantle of her famous father. Only ten at the time of his death, it took her a long time to come to terms with her turbulent upbringing, but through her friendship in adult life with family friends such as Fred and his wife Mary, she found affection and consistency. Though she grew to love her father's work and became a writer herself, being Dylan's daughter was not always easy. There were bitter and costly legal battles over the children's share of his estate. The steady growth in Dylan's posthumous income over the years is probably unprecedented for a poet, but how wisely it has been spent is an interesting question.

And what of Caitlin, Dylan's wife and the mother of his children? She wrote at least four accounts of their relationship, and while they are not factually reliable – she was a self-confessed alcoholic who often deluded herself about her motives and actions – her fierce spirit and passion for her husband, or at least the pure poet she wanted him to be, are unmistakable. Seeing her from a 21st-century, feminist standpoint and informed by modern ideas about parenting and the safeguarding of children casts her in a new light. Today, Caitlin would be perceived as a child raised by dysfunctional parents and the adolescent victim of a sexually predatory family friend. Her father abandoned his wife and young daughters for other women and Caitlin grew up with her mother and sisters in the truly Bohemian world of Augustus John and his promiscuous entourage. It left her craving love and attention, which she was beautiful and talented enough to deserve, but it was Dylan who got it all, and that enraged her. To paraphrase another twentieth-century poet, they fucked her up, her mum and dad.

And then of course there is the voice of Dylan himself. Poems like 'Fern Hill' and 'Do not go gentle into that good night' are much loved poetic bookends to his own life. When read aloud in his rich booming voice and recorded on vinyl, they changed the meaning of poetry for a whole generation. But there is so much more. Short stories like 'The Peaches' and 'The Outing' vividly and affectionately evoke the south-west Wales of his youth, while 'Reminiscences of Childhood' and 'Return Journey', just two of two hundred BBC broadcasts that he made or wrote, did the same for radio listeners. The countless letters he wrote demonstrate his incredible grip of tone and register, from briskly businesslike to passionate and pleading, as well as his beguiling ability to talk his way out of almost any tricky situation.

There are voices in the background too – the sing-song intonation of Swansea chatter in pubs and cafes, the incantatory 'hwyl' of Welsh preachers, the crescendo and diminuendo of male voice choirs. You can hear them all in Dylan's work, as you can hear the barking of farm dogs, the cry of seagulls and the flow of wind and water. You can see them too – Dylan's ability to conjure up visual images from the written and spoken word was second to none. These sights and sounds of the landscape of Swansea, Gower and rural west Wales – those of my own childhood – were equally loved by Fred and Dylan's other creative friends. Their motifs and images appear over and over again in their work.

> These were the woods the river and sea
>> Where a boy
> In the listening
> Summertime of the dead whispered the truth of his joy
> To the trees and the stones and fish in the tide.
>> And the mystery
>> Sang alive
> Still in the water and the singingbirds.

The words are from 'Poem in October', which, for Fred, was one of those that best expressed the man. Dylan was not always an easy person to love, and some of his poetry is hard to understand, but as the centenary celebrations of his birth in 2014 demonstrated, a reappraisal of his life and work was long overdue.

PART ONE

LONDON CALLING

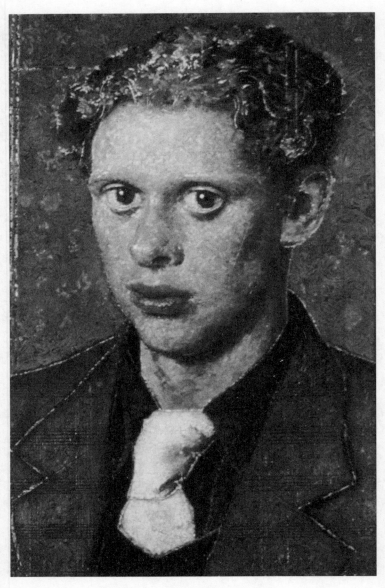

Dylan Thomas by Alfred Janes, 1934

CHAPTER ONE

A HAPPY SHAMBLES

The room in Earls Court had been let unfurnished, but the two young men who are sharing it have got hold of a couple of camp beds, a table and an oven which looks like a biscuit tin, placed over the solitary gas ring. The only chair has been modified for use as an easel, and on it one of the young men, Alfred Janes, is painting a portrait of his room-mate, a poet. His name is Dylan Thomas, he is twenty years old and the portrait is the first of three that Janes will make over the course of a friendship that lasts a lifetime.

The floor is scattered with beer bottles, fag ends and large pieces of cardboard covered in the poet's writing. As Janes works, Dylan explains the use of rhythm by the Victorian poet Gerard Manley Hopkins, his mouth stuffed full of jelly babies. While the finished portrait shows Dylan neatly, if unconventionally, dressed in a dark jacket and shirt and bright yellow tie, the unheated room is so cold on this winter day in 1934 that he is sitting in bed wearing a large checked overcoat and a pork pie hat to keep warm. Fred, as he is known to family and friends, is a meticulous painter who works slowly. He is developing a new technique of incising a grid-like pattern with a penknife over the finished work to give it a slightly raised, jewel-like quality. You can see it in the checks on the jacket in the portrait. But he knows he must make the most of his friend's presence – Dylan never stays put for long and will be in and out of their digs 'like a cat in a tripe shop'.

Fred had been living in London since 1931, moving up from

their hometown of Swansea when he won a scholarship from the art school there to study portraiture at the Royal Academy Schools in Piccadilly. It was also the year that he had met Dylan through another mutual friend, Daniel Jones, a brilliant young musician and composer. All three had been pupils at the grammar school in Swansea, where Dylan's father was a formidable English teacher. Fred had kept in touch when he went home for the summer holidays, or when Dylan began to make his first forays to London. Literary society in Swansea in the 1930s was somewhat limited, but in the capital the teenage poet could try to cultivate his contacts on the newspapers and magazines that were beginning to publish his work. The appearance of his first volume of poetry, *18 Poems*, at the end of 1934, was a golden opportunity to raise his profile.

At the Royal Academy Fred was surrounded by rare beings. Fellow student Peter Scott constructed models of birds – he was later to be knighted for his work as a wildlife conservationist and founder of bird sanctuaries. Another, Mervyn Peake, could transform a perfectly normal model in the life class into a prototype character from *Gormenghast*, the fantastical trilogy he would later write. 'Outside it was bleaker,' Fred recalled. 'It was soon after the Great Depression, money was scarce and the art students were all broke.' His parents, who owned a fruit and flower shop in Swansea, gave him £1 a week (a fraction of average earnings at the time), and Dylan's parents followed suit. They moved around in various combinations from one set of grotty digs to the next, which Fred described as an 'unfurnished but happy shambles'.

At one stage he and his fellow academy student William Scott moved into an unfurnished flat in Redcliffe Street in Earls Court, a rundown area of west London. It was some time before they acquired any furniture, and quite a while before they were to be seen carrying mattresses, picked up at knock-down sales on Fulham Road. On one occasion the landlady made an equally-broke fellow student a stew which he took in an iron saucepan on the bus from his digs in St John's Wood and carried down Bond Street to heat up and share in the academy's common room.

The painter William Scott by Alfred Janes, 1933.
A fellow Royal Academy Schools student,
they shared digs in London

Another student who was better off and lived upstairs from Fred and William in some style preferred their happy shambles to his well-appointed isolation, and soon moved in with a few luxuries including, much to Fred's delight, a collection of records: 'Schnabel playing Beethoven piano concertos; Mozart symphonies; that wonderful Bach double violin concerto and perhaps for us, even more revelatory, a broad introduction to more modern composers such as Ravel, Debussy, Scriabin, Prokofiev and Stravinsky. It was an intensely formative time, one of endless discussion,' Fred recalled. 'We were all immensely stimulated by the great artists of the period, from Picasso to Klee, from Gabo to Epstein.'

Life at the stuffy RA Schools was rather dull by comparison – students went there to work and then went home again, but fun and games were to be had at the unmissable Friday night hops at the Royal College of Art in Kensington, where other friends from Swansea and William's native Northern Ireland were studying. The glamorous annual Chelsea Arts Ball, held at the Royal Albert Hall, was not so easily accessible or affordable, however – until someone heard that its doors were not locked but held shut by powerful springs allowing exit but not entry, unless enough fingers could prise them open. Six students, including Fred and William, having practised first on similar doors, pulled off the feat and pelted up the stairs. 'It was a glorious night,' Fred said, 'but I have a strong feeling that for all of us, the climax was at the beginning and not the end.'

One weekend, a friend suggested that, if the tidal current was right, it was possible to row down the Thames from Richmond in Surrey to Limehouse in east London. A boat was duly hired and four of them, including Fred and William, made fair time until, near Tower Bridge, they met a series of barges moored side by side that blocked their progress. Unable to change direction in time, the hapless crew members were swept against them and had to force their way along to the end of the row by standing up and pushing above their heads against the barges. The more they pushed, the more they rocked and a long struggle ensued until they reached the last barge 'exhausted by a combination of effort, panic and hysterical laughter'. They managed to reach Limehouse, but missed the return tide and did not get back to the boathouse until the early hours of the following morning, where, Fred recalled, they were 'met with greetings entirely lacking in warmth'.

It was into this student world of art, music, crazy adventures and financial hardship that Dylan arrived in November 1934. Fred had decided to leave the academy by then, but he stayed on with the others for a short period painting in the flat. 'I was something of a factotum preparing our evening meals of vegetable stews etc. and wondering what on earth to do next. One was now highly trained, but not to earn one's living.' He returned to Swansea for a summer break and then took the flat in Redcliffe in Earls Court. 'I remember the journey up from Swansea well,' Fred recalled later. 'My parents drove us up, Dylan with one huge case, the pork pie hat and check overcoat like a marquee over his slight frame.

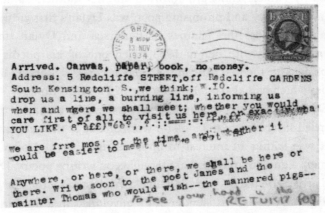

*A postcard sent from Dylan to a friend announcing his
arrival at Fred's digs in London, November 1934*

'Our room – or studio as it had become since I had left the academy and was painting on my own – seemed quite ordinary at the time, but when I thought back on it I was not surprised that it filled our parents – when they could steel themselves to visit – with utter dismay.' An iron bedstead which they had found made an admirable wardrobe when placed up on end against the wall, castors facing out and covered with a sort of curtain. As Fred was using the only chair as an easel, they sat on the camp beds. 'I remember one of these collapsing completely under Dylan's father on one of his visits. This horrified me. After all, to me Mr Thomas was still my erstwhile English master at the old school.' Dylan had spent all morning tidying up his room and it was in apple-pie order, according to his mother, Florence, with his books lined up neatly on the shelves. But they had to take it in turns to have a cup of tea in the sitting room and, she said, 'if there was one empty milk bottle, there were twenty'. They were at last able to all sit down at the same time when other odds and ends of furniture were lent to them by Pamela Hansford Johnson and her mother. Pamela, a young secretary and promising poet, was Dylan's first girlfriend. She lived across the Thames in Battersea and Dylan started corresponding with her in 1933 when one of his poems was published for the first time in the *Sunday Referee*, a London-based paper which had also published some of Pamela's work.

Dylan's first visits to London were ostensibly to stay with his married sister Nancy and look for work on one of the publications that was taking an interest in him. But they were also to visit Pamela – and not only to share thoughts on writing poetry. Dylan had arrived on the 21-year-old Pamela's doorstep for the first time in February 1934, his slender body enveloped in a mackintosh whose pockets were crammed with papers and poems, as well as a quarter bottle of brandy. Her description reveals how well Fred's portrait captures his boyish, but penetrating gaze – and how attractive Dylan was to her:

When he took off his pork pie hat (which he also told me later was what he had decided poets wore), he revealed a large and remarkable head – not shaggy, for he was visiting – but heavy with hair the dull gold of threepenny bits springing in deep waves and curls from a precise middle parting. His brow was very broad, not very high: his eyes the colour and opacity of caramels when he was solemn, the colour and transparency of sherry when he was lively, were very large and fine, and the lower rims rather heavily pigmented. His nose was a blob; his thick lips had a chapped appearance; a fleck of cigarette paper was stuck to the lower one. His chin was small and the disparity between the breadth of the lower and upper parts of his face gave an impression at the same time comic and beautiful. He looked like a brilliant, audacious child, and at once my family loved and fussed over him as if he were one.

Her reaction was probably already familiar to Dylan – and it was one that he was to arouse over and over again in many different women. When he returned to Swansea a few days later, he wrote and told Pamela that he loved her. There were more visits to London that year, and they enjoyed what Pamela described as 'a nice little affair', spending a holiday in Swansea, chaperoned by her mother, enjoying the spectacular scenery of the nearby Gower peninsula. The amount he drank sometimes worried her, and she was puzzled by the way that he would pretend in company to be much drunker than she knew he was. But soon after that first visit Dylan, still only nineteen, was to win the *Sunday Referee*'s 'Poet's Corner' prize, which guaranteed the publication of a volume of his poetry at the paper's expense. Pamela had won it the year before. It was the appearance of Dylan's *18 Poems* in December that year that had helped convince his parents that he should move to London, the respectable Mr Janes senior at the wheel, with the older, more sensible Fred to keep an eye on him in the big city.

Another young Swansea artist lived with them at 5 Redcliffe Street, Mervyn Levy. He was Dylan's oldest Swansea friend; they had met as seven-year-old pupils at Mrs Hole's, a little private junior school near their homes in the Swansea suburbs. Later, Mervyn had also attended the grammar school and then the art school. Here he met Fred, whose 1931 portrait of Mervyn helped him to win his scholarship to the RA Schools. He was now studying at the Royal College of Art. These three members of 'Swansea's Bohemia in exile', Dylan thought, were going to 'ring the bells of London and paint it like a tart'.

'We had some wonderful times together that have merged into a sort of kaleidoscopic image of laughter, arguments, experiments, quarrels and more laughter,' Fred wrote. 'Both Dylan and Mervyn could be enormously funny. We all took each other's work completely for granted. Although during this period, *18 Poems* was published with great success, I don't remember it making any difference to him or his endless comings and goings at all.'

Fred and Mervyn Levy washing up in the outdoor 'kitchen' at their digs in London, c.1933

Mervyn would often visit Dylan, who habitually slept fully clothed, at about nine in the morning. 'I would shake Dylan awake, hand him a cigarette and a light and wait for the first low rumble of coughing to build up to a shattering, purple-faced crescendo,' he recounted in a BBC broadcast. 'He always got the most out of his coughing fits … which he really enjoyed in a curious, perverse way. He liked to spread around the entirely romantic idea that he was dying of TB. The breakfast cigarette was a great help here…' Occasionally Dylan would vary the morning routine by reciting fragments of his poetry, such as these lines from 'The force that through the green fuse drives the flower', one of his *18 Poems*. Mervyn and Fred didn't know at the time that the power of its imagery was going to inspire many other artists and writers in years to come.

> The force that through the green fuse drives the flower
> Drives my green age; that blasts the root of trees
> Is my destroyer.
> And I am dumb to tell the crooked rose
> My youth is bent by the same wintry fever.

Dylan and Mervyn also loved to indulge in 'breakfast time fantasy weaving'. One morning Dylan started conjuring up an 'oilyverse' – a world where everything was dripping in oil. Mervyn visualised everyone slipping about all over the place. Not only that, Dylan pointed out – it would be horribly difficult to remain upright at all and everyone would have to address the Pope as 'His oiliness'. The number of mice required to pull the *Royal Scot* train from Edinburgh to London at 100 mph was the subject of another conundrum, and it was agreed that dwarfs with whips might be needed to keep them all galloping in line.

There were darker moments for Mervyn, who was Jewish. The years 1934 and 1935 were a period of great tension, already foreshadowing the Second World War. Oswald Mosley's British Union of Fascists, the 'Blackshirts', were making their presence felt on the streets of London, holding rallies which often ended in violent confrontations with communists and Jews. One evening Mervyn, Fred and William were to experience it first-hand. Mervyn enjoyed dressing in somewhat bizarre fashion – on this occasion in trousers slashed to the knee and one half of his face clean shaven, the other half bearded.

They were returning at night by tube from the West End to Earls Court, when a group of black-shirted youths began to taunt Mervyn. At the entrance to the tube station they met with a group of some thirty or forty Blackshirts – obviously on their way to a rally. 'They immediately surrounded us jostling and threatening,' recalled Fred. Fortunately the students' propensity for "endless discussion" came to their aid. 'It took what seemed an age to convince them that we were not "Trotsky's best friends". Mollified, eventually they went their way. That kind of confrontation was sadly all too frequent at the time.'

When they weren't indulging in banter or risky behaviour, work was a serious matter. 'In the flat Dylan did much of his writing and it was there above all that one learned how meticulous a craftsman he was,' Fred noted. None of them had enough money to buy anything apart from a little beer, and Dylan never drank when he was working. 'He would revise tirelessly and the room could be inundated with papers, gradually to be organised and collated and resulting frequently in a poem appearing complete and written out in his inimitable hand on a large sheet of card to be "seen" as well as read.'

One poem that particularly caught Fred's artist's eye was 'Vision and Prayer', although it wasn't published till much later. It forms a lozenge shape by starting off with one word in line one, then adding a word to each line until there are eight words, and then reversing the process until the last line consists of one word. Dylan's penchant, Fred believed, for experimenting with writing out his poems as word-shape compositions on these sheets of cardboard stemmed directly from his highly developed visual sense. Certainly, his ability to conjure up vivid pictures in the mind's eye of his readers was one of his most compelling skills.

This sensory connection to words was mirrored by Fred's tactile appreciation of his own medium. 'Paint has weight, it has substance. You buy it by the pound or by the tube. It has all sorts of aspects to it – its fluidity, its viscousness, its wateriness, its oiliness. It's a love of making things.'

And perhaps only an artist would make this observation:

In some early poems, Dylan's delight in mixing – deliberately – pure sound patterns with verbal clues and leaving the reader to 'get on with' the meaning was very akin, I feel, to Picasso's device of placing an eye here and a nose there and forcing the looker to get on with the face, which – being provided with these bits and pieces – the brain will not let him avoid.

Fred even suspected, controversially, that in his early work, Dylan was sometimes mischievously presenting the reader with a superbly constructed puzzle with no solution, 'knowing, diabolically, that it will be finally solved and that books will be written about the solution'.

The furious bursts of work that produced such poems would be interspersed with a complete disappearance from view, after which Dylan would often turn up with some new friend: a down-and-out from the Embankment, a broken-down American boxer, a communist in hiding from the fascists. They would stay for a while, maybe hours, days or weeks, then disappear for good. 'There must have been a strange contrast between our habits,' Fred remarked. 'Whereas I was glued to my easel-cum-chair experimenting away day after day, Dylan would disappear for days – perhaps weeks on end; on one occasion he went out to get a haircut and the next time I saw him was in Swansea.'

Dylan had always been restless, but perhaps this tendency to disappear was because, despite his eagerness to live in London, he liked neither the discomfort nor the cold of his digs. He was used to being molly-coddled by his mother and writing in the solitude of his suburban Swansea home, not with all the distractions of living at such close quarters with messy artists. Only a month after arriving he wrote to a Swansea friend complaining about the 'little maggots' he was living with and how boring and provincial he found them.

> I find it difficult to concentrate in a room as muddled and messy as ours is nearly all the time. For yards around me I see nothing but poems, poems, poems, mashed potatoes, mashed among my stories and Janes' canvasses. One day we shall have to wash up, and then perhaps I can really begin to work.

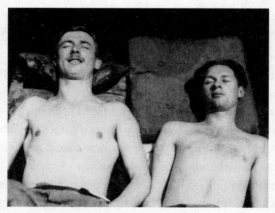

Fred Janes and Dylan Thomas sunbathing on the
roof of 5 Redcliffe Street in London, c.1935
photographed by William Scott

Another reason for Dylan's comings and goings was that he was spending much of his time with a rapidly growing circle of friends and admirers, developing relationships that were later to help him earn a living by book reviewing, broadcasting on BBC radio, writing film scripts, not to mention promoting and publishing his own work. And of course there were all the temptations of London's Bohemian quarters in Soho and Fitzrovia. Dylan and Fred would occasionally meet for coffee in the Lyons Corner House, or, if funds permitted, a bowl of spaghetti in Bertorelli's restaurant. But it was in pubs and clubs like the Fitzroy Tavern in Charlotte Street or, after it shut at about 10 p.m., the arty Gargoyle club in Dean Street, that Dylan charmed his fellow drinkers with brilliant impersonations and shaggy dog stories. And it was in the Wheatsheaf Tavern, off Tottenham Court Road, that he would meet the love of his life, Caitlin Macnamara – a relationship that turned out to be so mutually destructive and almost broke the bonds with his old Swansea friends.

Fred and Dylan soon moved on, this time to Coleherne Road, round the corner from Redcliffe Street, where William Scott joined them again. Fred said later that it was here that he painted the 1934 portrait of Dylan – if so he must have done it uncharacteristically quickly, as Dylan had been living with him in Redcliffe Street only since November. Perhaps Dylan had sat for Fred on some of his earlier visits to London, before moving up officially. But wherever it was done, their surroundings would have been just as happy and shambolic. According to Mervyn, Fred was in charge of collecting the rent, and while Dylan only had a mattress to sleep on, if he didn't pay his share, Fred, who was much taller and stronger, would pick him up, turn him upside down and shake him till any loose change fell out of his trouser pockets. Dylan's habit of leaving his bed full of cake crumbs and apple cores was another source of irritation to Fred, who was a marginally tidier creature.

21

Fred painted a second portrait of Mervyn here in 1935 and because he was studying art himself, unlike Dylan he knew how to sit patiently, much to Fred's relief.

By now Fred was developing the idea of the simple grid pattern visible on Dylan's jacket in the 1934 portrait into a highly organised framework with very ordered geometry. He was moving away from the traditional idea of painting and drawing as a means of representing the world around him to experimenting with the ingredients of painting – colour, line and shape. While his chosen medium was different from Dylan's, their desire to conjure in this way with line and shape – and in the poet's case, sound – was closely connected and reflected a powerful Modernist streak in their outlook.

But Fred's new ideas didn't fit in with the traditional teaching at the RA, excellent though it was, and despite the fact that he had been a model pupil. By the end of his first year in 1931, as the local paper in Swansea proudly reported, he had won first prizes of £5 each for life drawing, head studies and painting from the antique, as well as three monthly prizes for composition, and in 1932 he won the Royal Academy of Arts Prize Medal for figure drawing. But by 1934 life drawing classes – which he had been attending by now for about seven years – were beginning to pall and he was by then a highly accomplished draughtsman. He started skipping a few daytime classes to study Chinese painting at the British Museum or fossils at the Natural History Museum and modern masters like Braque, Klee and Kandinsky in the Cork Street commercial galleries a stone's throw from the RA.

Academy classes were in the evening as well as during the morning, and Fred had been absent from some of the daytime sessions. As he was going in one evening, he met the Keeper (principal) of the Royal Academy Schools, Sir Walter Russell, a traditional painter of landscapes and portraits in the Victorian mould. 'We haven't seen much of you recently, Janes,' Sir Walter said sternly. When Fred explained that he had been studying in art galleries and museums, Sir William retorted: 'We don't cater for part-timers here.' 'It was Picasso v Sir Walter Russell,' Fred explained. 'Picasso won.'

By the summer of 1935 the ménage at Coleherne Road had broken up. All three met up over the next year or so in Cornwall, where William and Fred had gone to paint, and Dylan to recuperate from the excesses of London life. Weekly dances in Penzance were not to be missed, but for Fred this meant walking the ten miles back to St Ives, where he was staying, fuelled by 3 a.m. cheese and onion sandwiches eaten in a hedgerow to keep him going.

Fred went back to Swansea for the holidays, thinking he would return to London. But he didn't, and all four years' worth of his RA drawings and paintings, which he had left in the flat, were nearly lost. Luckily for him, the influential artists Augustus John and Cedric Morris (who was also from Swansea) were organising an exhibition by Welsh painters in Cardiff, and wanted to include paintings by Fred that they had seen in a one-man show held at the Everyman Cinema in Hampstead, so Fred had gone up to London to fetch them. Two were subsequently bought for £15 each by the National Museum and Gallery of Wales in Cardiff – a still life, *Bream*, and the portrait of Dylan – which hang there to this day.

*Swansea, Thomas' hometown 'by the side of
a long and splendid curving shore'*

CHAPTER TWO

AN UGLY, LOVELY TOWN

Dylan and Fred now met mostly in Swansea, where Dylan still spent a lot of time, and Fred was back at home with his parents. Oddly enough he saw much more of Dylan than he did when they were sharing digs in London. Swansea – Dylan's 'ugly, lovely town' – was very much a place of two halves. Set on the sweeping curve of Swansea Bay, it offered safe anchorage for big ships that sailed up the Bristol Channel and docked at the mouth of the river Tawe on the east side of the town. The Welsh name for Swansea, Abertawe, means 'mouth of the Tawe'. From further up the steeply sided valley came plentiful coal supplies, helping Swansea to thrive first as a centre for coal export and copper smelting in the eighteenth century, earning it the nickname 'Copperopolis', then fuelling its expansion as a hub of the industrial revolution.

This side of town, with its terraced housing for factory and dock workers and the seedy attractions of the port, was where Dylan's mother, Florence, one of eight children, was born in a cramped house near the docks. Her father worked as an inspector there and was a deacon of the local Congregational chapel and superintendent of the Sunday school. Welsh speaking, like Florence's mother, he was born in rural Carmarthenshire, where relatives still lived on smallholdings on the pretty Llansteffan peninsula, about thirty miles west of Swansea. Laugharne, to be made famous by their future son, was a short ferry ride away across the Taf river estuary.

Chapel and the Carmarthenshire countryside were also part of Dylan's father's upbringing. Jack Thomas was born and raised in a cottage on the outskirts of Carmarthen, the county town, where his father worked on the railways. As was so often the case in Wales, education offered an escape from working-class life. Jack, a bright boy, won a place at the University of Aberystwyth to study English and train as a teacher. He wrote poetry and contributed to student magazines, sang and belonged to the Music Society. On graduation, he was the only student in Wales to be awarded a first-class honours degree in English that year.

Any hopes he had of pursuing an academic or literary career seemed to fade, however, and from 1901 until his retirement he was an English master at Swansea Grammar School. Soon after taking up the post, he met Florence – perhaps in Swansea or when both of them happened to be visiting relatives who lived near each other in Carmarthenshire. They married in 1903, possibly, according to local gossip, because Florence was pregnant (they were, unusually, not married by her brother-in-law, a preacher at the family's usual chapel), but whatever the reason, they united all the influences that were to mould Dylan, and, in fact, all his Swansea friends – rural Welsh roots, class division, upward mobility and a love of learning – literature and music especially. The newly-built house that Florence and Jack moved into eleven years later with their daughter Nancy at 5 Cwmdonkin Drive was a few miles but a world away from the factories and docks of Swansea. The genteel suburbs to the west of the town wend their way across steep slopes with expansive views across the wide sweep of Swansea Bay to the pretty little seaside village of Mumbles. It was, Dylan wrote later in 'Reminiscences of Childhood', 'an ugly, lovely town (or so it was, and is, to me), crawling, sprawling, slummed, unplanned, jerry villa'd and smug-suburbed by the side of a long and splendid-curving shore...'

Their son Dylan was born in the best upstairs bedroom on 27 October 1914. He was named after a character in *The Mabinogion*, a collection of medieval Welsh myths, but Dylan was pronounced in the English way and not 'Dullan', as it would be in Welsh. The name was unheard of until it was chosen for him. So here was a boy with his feet in two very different cultural camps from the word go. The cough that was to accompany Mervyn's offering of morning tea in Redcliffe Street many years later started early. A slight boy with a halo of golden curls, Dylan was thought to have asthma, and at the first sign of a wheeze was wrapped up warm by Florence, who fretted about TB, or tucked up in bed in his tiny room with bread soaked in warm milk – comfort food that her precious boy would never grow out of. Across the road from the house was Cwmdonkin Park, where Dylan climbed trees, played pranks and acted out boyhood fantasies. Memories of these days and the Swansea of his childhood would be beautifully evoked decades later in his poem 'The hunchback in the park' and 'Reminiscences of Childhood', a BBC radio broadcast.

> And the park itself was a world within the world of the sea town; quite near where I lived, so near that on summer evenings I could listen, in my bed, to the voices of other children playing ball on the sloping, paper-littered bank; the park was full of terrors and treasures. The face of one old man who sat, summer and winter, on the same bench looking over the swanned reservoir, I can see more clearly than the city street faces I saw an hour ago...

Dylan's schooldays began when he joined Nancy at a small private establishment run by a Mrs Hole in her house a few minutes' walk down the hill. Here she prepared the children whose parents could afford the fees to enter the town's best secondary schools, with a traditional curriculum sandwiched between bible reading and hymns in the morning and reading aloud in the afternoon. Dylan played on all the senses to vividly recreate it in 'Reminiscences of Childhood'. It was:

> ...so firm and kind and smelling of galoshes, with the sweet and fumbled music of the piano-lessons drifting down from upstairs to the lonely schoolroom where only sometimes the tearful wicked sat over undone sums or to repent a little crime – the pulling of a girl's hair during geography, the sly shin-kick under the table during prayers.

Dylan excelled at reading aloud, especially when he could choose a poem to recite. Like many children of Swansea parents who were keen to climb the social ladder, he attended elocution lessons to clip the broad vowels and sing-song intonation of a south Wales accent. The skinny little boy with a halo of golden curls and big brown eyes was a born actor who loved making mischief and being the centre of attention. A fellow former pupil at Mrs Hole's recalled how he ruined a performance of *Macbeth* by putting a stink bomb in the witches' cauldron. Little did she know that this *enfant terrible* with beautiful diction, a gift for reading poetry aloud and getting himself noticed would become not just a great poet himself, but an innovative radio broadcaster and live performer with huge popular appeal.

On Saturday afternoons there were matinées at the local cinema, known as the 'bug house', where Dylan developed a love of the genre that would eventually take him to Hollywood. Westerns, Charlie Chaplin and later the Marx Brothers were all favourites – accompanied by endless wine gums – and his brilliant capacity for mimicry must have been honed in part in the Uplands fleapit. His love of acting continued when he started at the grammar school in 1925. He played several leading roles including, incongruously for his small stature and angelic curls, Oliver Cromwell. Attempts to improve the likeness were hampered by the false wart that kept slipping off his face. Fortunately his acting ability made up for his lack of height, and he was singled out for praise for this and other roles in reviews in the local paper, the *South Wales Daily Post* (later *Evening Post*). Surprisingly too, for a boy of less than average height, whose mother fretted about his weak chest, he could beat much older boys at running on sports days – not something he would mention when playing the part of the romantic poet with TB in later life.

But Dylan's main interests at school were writing poetry, debating motions like 'Modern Youth is Decadent' at the society he initiated and producing, sometimes single-handedly, the school magazine, in which his first published poem appeared. These pursuits were to the exclusion of all other academic subjects, for which Dylan had little time. One of his classmates, Charlie Fisher, recalled how he reacted to a furious maths teacher hurling abuse at the class. 'Dylan stood up and said "Sir, I do not wish to learn mathematics in your class," picked up his books and walked out. It was an inconceivable act of courage to the other boys.' Dylan never went to maths lessons after that. At home his father would be pleased to see through a little glass panel in the door to his study that Dylan was doing his homework, only to find later that a shuffle of papers under the homework book gave the game away. He was writing poetry instead.

Later on, when the senior boys had access to their own study with a coal fire, Fisher recalled Dylan using the red hot poker not to toast crumpets but to try and bore a hole through the wooden floor into the masters' room below. The two were almost exact contemporaries and Charlie shared Dylan's love of English, skipping classes with him on the pretext of working on the school magazine. 'We collected words like entomologists collected moths or butterflies. Dan Jones would invent phrases like "metrical biscuitry", Dylan would mutter it tasting the sound, not looking for any meaning.' Charlie also enjoyed acting and they played a married couple in a school production of John Galsworthy's *Strife*, Dylan taking the lead role, appropriately, of a strike leader, while Charlie played his wife. Sometimes they would cut school completely and sit in the Kardomah Cafe in town. 'We would talk about girls as though they were an altogether separate species from ourselves, Welsh culture being founded on this proposition,' Charlie recollected.

Dylan's attitude at school was a source of embarrassment to Thomas senior, who was now senior English master and known by his initials D.J. rather than the chummier Jack. Dylan's enthusiasm for English, however, meant that his father turned a blind eye to his son's poor performance in other subjects, his frequent absences and truanting. D.J. 'combined hauteur with an acid turn of speech,' which, according to Charlie, 'intimidated colleagues who actually enjoyed their jobs and were wary of challenging him'. Florence had another explanation. She later told Fred that if teachers remonstrated with Dylan it would trigger an asthma attack and he would be sent home from school and need a week off to recover. So they stopped telling him off. D.J.'s study in Cwmdonkin Drive was lined with books and he knew, after all, how much time Dylan spent there. 'My education', Dylan said, 'was the liberty I had to read indiscriminately and all the time, with my eyes hanging out.' D.J. also had a beautiful speaking voice and would read aloud to Dylan, especially when Florence had tucked the sickly boy up in bed at the onset of another wheeze, or kept him indoors away from the drizzle that drifts in from the Atlantic and can wrap Swansea in its damp embrace for days on end. Florence's voice also had range and power and she could recount the tittle-tattle of the day with great verve – qualities that her son inherited.

If D.J. tolerated his son's failings, he was less lenient towards other pupils. Frustrated by his teaching career and bored after so long at the same school, he was not a happy teacher. Fred, being several years older, did not meet Dylan until after they had left the grammar school, but his first-hand experience of D.J. meant he recognised his significance in Dylan's development. 'He savoured words and poetry as other people savour food and drink and from his earliest childhood Dylan was totally immersed in a sea of language.' As far as Fred was concerned, D.J. could not have planted the seeds of his own passion for English in more fertile ground.

Fred was also all too familiar with D.J.'s moods. 'He read to us totally disregarding the hellish mixture of tedium, indifference, fidgeting and scorn that can be created only by boys in school. Listening was urgent, compulsory. I can hear him now,' Fred wrote decades later. 'Once or twice I saw him reach the point of exasperation and he would explode into a really violent mood; somebody would catch it – hard – and there would be a few minutes of truce.' Such angry outbursts were also displayed by Dylan, who despite his girlish physique would tackle playground bullies, and when he was old enough to drink, challenge people he found pompous or patronising. Another fellow pupil described D.J. as 'being like a well-camouflaged tiger, proud and prowling through the jungle of schoolboys'. This was Dan Jones, who had become Dylan's closest friend after their first encounter started with a scrap, an episode on which Dylan later based his autobiographical short story 'The Fight'. It opens with Dylan trying to goad a neighbour into losing his temper.

I had almost beaten him, the newspaper was trembling, he was breathing heavily, when a strange boy, whom I had not heard approach, pushed me down the bank.

31

I threw a stone at his face. He took off his spectacles, put them in his coat pocket, took off his coat, hung it neatly on the railings, and attacked.

Dylan and Dan were in the same year at the grammar school but their home lives were very different. By the time Dylan had started secondary school Nancy, who was six years older, was a young lady more interested in men of her own age than her little brother and his endless sheets of paper filled with poems. Once, when he asked her what he could write about, she suggested, sarcastically, the kitchen sink. Florence recalled that it was rather a good poem, along with another one about an onion.

D.J. was as broody at No. 5 as he was in school, spending the evenings in his study doing the *Times* crossword or reading, or lingering over a stout in the pub. Perhaps he found his possible shotgun marriage to Florence as disappointing as his job. A warm, maternal woman, she had left her position as a seamstress in a department store and had few interests beyond keeping house and looking after her family. Childhood friends of Dylan were welcomed warmly at Cwmdonkin Drive and enjoyed her home-baked teas, while D.J. could be more aloof. Her husband, she explained to Dan's mother, was 'very nervous' and had enough of young boys during the day, preferring to be left to his own devices in the evening. D.J. did not always leave his temper behind at school, however, and would sometimes lash out at the family, prompting Nancy on one occasion to run away and stay with her aunt on the Llansteffan peninsula.

The atmosphere at Dan's house could not have been more different. A short walk away from Cwmdonkin Drive in Eversley Road in Sketty, another genteel suburb further towards the Gower peninsula in the west, Warmley was a spacious Victorian villa inhabited by very different creatures. Dan's father was a bank

32

manager, but also a composer, mainly of church music. An adjudicator at the Eisteddfodau, the ancient Welsh festivals of music and poetry, he would entertain the family with anecdotes about his travels around Wales and the people he met. He had read widely in French and German, was interested in astrology and astronomy and wrote lectures on topics as diverse as 'Religion in Renaissance Painting' and 'The Harmony of the Universe'.

To Dan 'he was the funniest man I ever knew, with the possible exception of Dylan himself'. A very funny man indeed in that case.

Dan's mother sang, played the piano and was a highly accomplished needlewoman whose tapestries were exhibited in London. Dan and his older brother Jim, also an able musician, were at first taught at home from the age of five by his mother's cousin, 'Aunt Alice', who followed a strict regime including musical composition. Dan wrote the first of his, 'The Moon', aged four. It is hardly surprising that in this spirited, cultured atmosphere, young Jones was a polymath in the making, whom Dylan sent up gently in 'The Fight'. 'He was a composer and a poet too; he had written seven historical novels before he was twelve, and he played the piano and the violin ... He showed me his books and his seven novels. All the novels are about battles, sieges and kings. "Just early stuff," he said.'

Once at the grammar school, where the teachers were not always as accomplished as Aunt Alice, Dan would occasionally join Dylan in one of his 'mitching' episodes and spend the day in Cwmdonkin Park, where they would read and write poetry. Dan sometimes visited No. 5, but Warmley was a far more appealing environment for lively boys. It soon became Dylan's second home, where he could indulge in his love of creating elaborate fantasies. Unlike Dan, he could not play the piano – 'I can do chords, not tunes' – but this was no barrier to performing with Dan and other school friends like Tom Warner. Their instruments included a piano, two violins, a cello and two recorders, plus a percussion section made of biscuit tins and an old motor horn. A snapshot of their imaginary musical world is captured in Dan's memoir, *My Friend Dylan Thomas*.

> A whole mythology of composers, instrumentalists and singers was invented; some of the heroes of this mythology were … Winter Vaux, X.Q. Xumn, Lacketty Apps and above all the Reverend Percy who dominated the musical scene with his innumerable piano pieces. Opera was not forgotten. In this medium the great composer was X.Q. Xumn, whose principal opera, *Blacker Moon* … consisted of 400 scenes, some of which were complete operas in themselves; one scene in Act Two for example, consisted of Bizet's *Carmen*.

Less ambitious 'chamber' pieces were performed with each player allowed only one note of his instrument at a time, with the turns regulated to a strict predetermined pattern. This system of taking turns was also implemented in Dan and Dylan's literary collaborations, when they would write alternate lines of poems under the pen name Walter Bram. Sometimes these were 'hat poems', for which they wrote individual lines on separate pieces of paper which they then randomly pulled out of a hat. The results could be striking, if totally nonsensical.

> Hurrah! cones for our small meal!
> One per cent of public moth.

Tom Warner was another musically gifted grammar school boy. Thanks to him, the WBC (Warmley Broadcasting Corporation) was launched from the upstairs drawing room, where he wired up loudspeakers that acted as microphones linked to the radiogram in the downstairs sitting room (or so Dan, who, unlike Tom, was not very technically minded, understood). At its inaugural broadcast, Dan's father was sitting comfortably next to the radiogram when Dylan asked if he could tune into some foreign radio stations. Mr Jones was unaware that he was in fact tuning into the WBC studio upstairs. At first he was delighted to hear Beethoven's 'Waldstein' sonata wafting across the airwaves, but then the pianist began to introduce discordant notes and chords until it became a 'farrago of sound' and certainly not Beethoven. Dylan recounted later to Dan and Tom how a red-faced Mr Jones leapt out of his chair and called out to his wife: 'Ettie! Listen to this! The world has gone mad!' His son was soon rumbled as the pianist playing upstairs – much to the amusement of his father, who became a regular WBC performer himself. The WBC also broadcast poetry readings – usually two-person scenes from Shakespeare, so the audience of one could listen downstairs. These would later be subject to strict criticism. When Dylan started working at the BBC as scriptwriter and broad-caster several years later, he had already had plenty of practice.

Fred entered the extraordinary world of Warmley in 1931. Dylan's father had by now given up all hope of his son proving his worth academically and found him a job as a reporter on the local paper, the *South Wales Daily Post*. Dylan left school at sixteen with only one qualification – in English. He made a laudable attempt to replace the school magazine as an outlet for his talents by trying to launch a subscription-based literary publication, but his plans foundered when he spent the first £10 donated on beer. Dan, by contrast, was set to become a brilliant student of English at Swansea University and graduate with a first-class degree, while Fred was studying art.

Fred spent his early years living over his father's fruit and flower shop in the centre of Swansea – his heritage in still life painting as he later described it. A child who was never happier than with paper and pencils or hammer and nails, he spent hours drawing and painting the produce in the shop, his father's cars – very useful, he realised later, for dealing with perspective – and portraits, for which he seemed to have a natural gift. The Janes family were well-established tradespeople in the town. 'J.G. Janes Florist and Fruiterer, Wreaths At Short Notice From 7s/6d,' their letterhead boasted – no lowly vegetables, mind. His mother was a canny businesswoman, her husband belonged to the Freemasons and their extended family worshipped every Sunday at York Place Baptist Chapel – an experience that turned Fred into a lifelong atheist. Family holidays with uncles, aunts and cousins were spent at the splendid Metropole Hotel in Llandrindod Wells, the largest in Wales when it was completed in 1846, where the family enjoyed taking part in bowls tournaments.

Like Dylan, Fred was not a success at school, partly, as he only discovered as a teenager, because he was very short-sighted and could not see the board. After leaving he went to Gregg's Commercial College, with a view to working in the family business. But he took evening classes at Swansea School of Art and in 1927 won a scholarship to study full time. 'The teaching there was very traditional and sound enough, but really belonged to the nineteenth century,' he said. Then a new exciting young teacher, George Cooper Mason, arrived from the Royal College of Art, who took his students up to London to visit art galleries. 'He was wonderful. He brought a totally new attitude of mind and it was all very enlightening.'

Swansea's '*crachach*' – the Welsh equivalent of the 'the great and the good' – were soon commissioning young Janes to paint their portraits. *The Cambrian Daily Leader* used one of them to illustrate their report in 1929 of a talk by Mr G. Oliver Luff to the Rotary

Club. It was about building societies, 'of which he has considerable experience in Swansea'. The paper proudly noted that Mr Luff's portrait would be one of four by Alfred Janes to be shown at a forthcoming exhibition at the Cardiff Art Society.

In 1929 Mervyn Levy joined Fred at the art school in Swansea and two years later he sat for the portrait that would win Fred his RA scholarship. But before he left for London, Dan invited Fred to Warmley to meet Dylan, and they soon began to think of themselves as a group. 'We spent many happy hours together whenever the opportunity arose, discussing our work and thrashing out our ideas when I was in Swansea on vacation, but I found the time as stimulating in every way as being in London, which was, of course, as exciting an experience as one could wish.'

Fred had learned to play the piano as a child – though he preferred to improvise – and was a very active member of the Warmley orchestra.

> We all played together on the piano, on any available instruments, on the plates, pots, pans and washboards. I think we felt, Dylan especially, that a certain element of pandemonium was an essential ingredient of civilised behaviour. There is no doubt that the counterpoint he practised with fire irons and coal scuttle takes on a forcefulness not easily forgotten.

Dan introduced Fred and Dylan to music in a way that only a composer could. He played for them – the piano, cello or violin – and would explain whatever interested them in the most detailed way, breaking it down phrase by phrase, note by note, until, Fred at least, really grasped the structure. Dan thought that artists and sculptors were more likely to appreciate music than writers, because they could accept that something significant could be conveyed by means other than words. Fred in turn was astonished at Dan's perception of sound. 'He could stand outside a room behind a closed door and if you struck ten random notes on a piano he would identify them all correctly immediately – provided the piano also had perfect pitch.'

It was fun but it also had a tremendous impact on Fred's work. While they all practised different arts – poetry, music, painting – they all learned from each other. 'One kind of artist understands another because he understands some of the possibilities and the potential, the problems and limitations of the medium in which he works, and he understands these because they parallel the characteristics of his own medium,' Fred explained.

> Paintings are made of paint, of shapes, of colours, of tonality and texture and they in turn precipitate the reaction of evocation, portrayal and communication.
>
> Poetry is made of words, the spoken word is heard but not seen, the written word is seen but is silent; the spoken word is sound and the written word is shape. Shape and sound call out in the reader, the listener, their meaning. Of these three kinds of magic Dylan was master. Every letter of the alphabet was to him a performance; it began, it developed and it drew to a close; it had pitch, volume and duration; it also had shape; even alone it was full of meaning. Words were sustained pieces, full of form and cadence. Lines and sentences offered a thousand alternative possibilities of structure, imagery and association. The particular music in Dylan's poetry springs spontaneously and directly from his acute sense of the reality of words as 'things' quite apart from their meanings.

Dylan, Dan and Fred talked and argued endlessly about these notions, and these early discussions, combined with their grasp of the pure craftsmanship that underpinned all their different arts, were a formative influence on their future achievements.

If D.J. had hoped that Dylan would make more of a success of his job at the paper than of his time at school, he was disappointed. Dylan spent the first few weeks at the *South Wales Daily Post* learning the ropes with routine tasks to which all rookie journalists are assigned. The tedium of proofreading was soon alleviated by writing doggerel on the back of the galley sheets, or when reading out copy for the typesetters, dramatising it in a booming voice, much to their annoyance. He was promoted to reporter, but his lack of shorthand meant he only covered – if he turned up – tedious council meetings, funerals and sports fixtures, or made routine enquiries at the police station, morgue and docks for the latest shipping news. Mostly he spent the time daydreaming, playing billiards at the YMCA or chatting in the toilets when 'I should have been writing up last night's performance of *The Crucifixion* or loitering, with my new hat on one side, through the Christmas-Saturday crowds.'

Dylan may have had 'almost every quality of a bad newspaper-man. Accuracy meant nothing to him; punctuality meant less,' according to one senior colleague, but the chance to escape the office and wander around Swansea looking for stories, dropping into cafes and pubs and observing everyday life in the town fed his remarkable powers of observation with raw material that would resurface later in colourful, evocative broadcasts and autobiographical short stories like 'Old Garbo'.

I made my way through the crowds: the Valley men, up to the football; the country shoppers, the window gazers; the silent, shabby men at the corners of the packed streets, standing in isolation in the rain; the press of mothers and prams; old women in black, brooched dresses carrying frails, smart girls

with shining mackintoshes and splashed stockings; little dandy
lascars, bewildered by the weather; business men with their wet
spats; through a mushroom forest of umbrellas; and all the time
I thought of the paragraphs I would never write. I'll put you
all in a story by and by.

If Dylan disliked office life, he relished the chance to sample low
life around the docks, where prostitutes, homosexuals, miners and
sailors congregated in the area's pubs. 'Old Garbo' describes how
a senior reporter on the *Tawe News* took teenage Dylan on a pub
crawl one evening, starting at the Three Lamps, across the road
from the paper. The cub reporter was clearly impressed by this
seasoned older hack and his perpetual cigarette, 'a hanging badge
of bad habits'. He also developed a taste for the watery Welsh beer
served in the dockside pubs. 'I liked the taste of beer, its live white
lather, its brass bright depths, the sudden world through the wet
brown walls of the glass...' The story didn't have a happy ending:
'Who kept filling my glass? Beer ran down my cheek and my collar,
my mouth was full of saliva. The bench span.' He spent his bus
fare home and crept upstairs to 'a wild bed, and the wallpaper lakes
converged and sucked me down'. The hangover was monstrous
enough to convince him he would never drink again, but it was all
bravado in the office on Monday morning.

Dylan's old school friend Charlie Fisher joined Dylan on the
Post, where his father was head printer. They were soon bunking
off again to chat to their literary and artistic friends in the
Kardomah Cafe near the newspaper's offices, making sure first that
they would not be spotted by one customer in particular – the
paper's manager. While Charlie described Dylan as 'looking like
an unmade bed', he was quite the dandy himself. Fred captured
his dapper good looks and neat moustache in a pencil portrait –
although without his customary monocle. A lover of the great

outdoors and a keen horseman, he often went riding if someone would lend him a mount. Once he failed to return it in time to get to work and decided to tie the animal up outside the paper's office and stride in wearing full riding habit. 'Where's your horse then, Charlie?' asked one wag. Knowing this was coming, Charlie took great delight in pointing through the window and replying: 'Over there'.

Highlights of Swansea's lively social calendar were commemorative dinners and annual dances held by local societies. There was the Caledonian Ball, the Hospital Ball, the Hunt Ball and even one hosted by the fishing club, known grandly as the Piscatorial Society (of which, as an expert angler with his own fishing column in the paper, Charlie was a member). Dressed up in top hat and tails, he must have cut quite a dash on the dance floor.

Despite all these distractions, Charlie took his work more seriously than Dylan and was thought very promising. This, combined with his undoubted journalistic talent, assured him a successful career, but Dylan's newspaper story had a different ending. The kind of work they were expected to produce, Charlie observed, cramped the poet's style. 'It was as if some world-famous *coloratura* had been asked to sing 'Roll Out the Barrel'. After barely sixteen months at the *Post* his alleged faux pas included forgetting to make a routine call to the fire station so that the paper missed the important news of a fire at the local hospital; failing to call on the hospital and discover that the matron had died suddenly; and running a report of a sports event that had, in fact, been cancelled. At the end of 1932 he left 'by mutual agreement' with the editor. The future might have looked bleak to most young men who left school at sixteen with barely any qualifications, then failed to hold down their first job, but Dylan felt nothing but relief, as he wrote to a friend: 'What I feared was the slow but sure stamping out of individuality, the gradual contentment with life as it was, so much per week, so much for this, for that, and so much left over for drink and cigarettes. That be no loife for such as Oi!' He had nothing to fear – his life could not have been more different.

There was still enough goodwill towards the errant cub reporter at the paper for it to publish freelance contributions from Dylan, as did its weekend sister paper, the *Herald of Wales*. Dylan also filed 'seasonal and snappy titbits' for various titles in the Northcliffe stable. His output consisted mostly of lighter pieces and funny verse, but a series on the poets of Swansea caused further consternation when one of them turned up at the paper's office outraged by Dylan's critical comments, which accused him of writing in derivative clichés. E. Howard Harris, who was also a schoolmaster, had not taken kindly to being dismissed by one so young. Dylan also claimed to have caused a libel suit by calling the flamboyant Bohemian author and painter Nina Hamnett insane and claiming that her autobiography had been banned. In fact the paper made a climb down before she instigated legal action. As he told the same friend: 'I am attempting to earn a living now – attempting is the correct word – by freelance journalism.'

While Dylan may have idled away his days as a reporter, at home he had been writing compulsively, filling notebooks with poetry. Now he would have more time to devote to his passion, but there was another outlet for his talents: the theatre. Devout chapelgoers in 1930s Swansea still saw the theatre as a little sinful, and people like Dylan Thomas and his arty crowd as rather 'advanced'. With no television, entertainment consisted of the pubs – which were only open for a few hours at lunchtime and in the evening, and closed on Sundays in Wales – the cinema and weekly dances, if there was money to spare. The town's young intellectuals and aspiring thespians were not satisfied by the popular fare at the local commercial theatre in any case, so to put on more serious plays by writers like Chekhov, Ibsen and

Shakespeare, they founded their own: the Swansea Little Theatre. Dan Jones was a member and often wrote the score or played music to accompany productions. In 1932 it found a new recruit. Dylan had satisfied his love of acting with minor parts in productions at the YMCA, but the Little Theatre offered more than the chance to indulge – it was a good place to meet the opposite sex. His sister Nancy was already a member, and had met her boyfriend Haydn there (away from Florence's prying eyes in Cwmdonkin Drive). They would not be the only couple to meet at its headquarters in a church school hall in Mumbles. One evening Fred came to see Dylan perform and fell for a very pretty young woman with rich auburn curls and soft brown eyes. Mary Ross would be his future wife, and my mother.

Dylan loved to flirt and make the girls blush with his smutty schoolboy humour and witty literary puns. He addressed one young actress in a low cut dress as '*Tess of the two big villes*' and sometimes wrote 'C.B.' in the margin of programmes – for Chastity Belt, meaning that they rejected his advances. Mary's sister Ethel Ross (later my aunt) was also a very active member of the theatre and wrote an account of Dylan's time as a member, *Dylan and Thomas and the Amateur Theatre*. 'He was not terribly male or adult,' she said. 'I thought of him as a bit of a midge, but he had a coy, ingratiating way with women.' Of his acting ability, however, she was in no doubt, and having seen him in several productions, remarked how versatile he was.

His progress as an amateur thespian followed the by-now familiar pattern of triumph and disaster. In February and April 1932, Dylan took lead roles in Noël Coward's *Hay Fever* alongside Nancy and Haydn, and in *The Beaux' Stratagem*, George Farquhar's Restoration romp. His performances were singled out for praise in the *Mumbles Press* and in the *Post* by his former editor, J.D. Williams – especially his role in *Peter and Paul* by H.F. Rubenstein, which traces the lives of two men from youth to old age. Dylan had lobbied hard to stage it, mainly, it emerged, for the chance of a star part. He played Peter, a frustrated writer who was forced to work in his father's business, only to feel haunted in later life by the books he never wrote. If the story reflected D.J.'s own lack of literary achievement, the same would not be true of his son.

In 1933 a Mrs Bertie Perkins hosted a production of *Electra*, Sophocles' tragic account of a daughter's revenge for the death of her beloved father, in the garden of her mansion in Sketty, the posh Swansea suburb adjoining the Uplands. Dan composed the music for harp and drums and Ethel had a walk-on part as well as being wardrobe and prop mistress (which included constantly topping up a bowl of fruit that mysteriously kept disappearing during the week-long run). One evening she noticed Dylan leaning on a tree, wearing the ubiquitous cigarette and looking very bored. But a few days later, the *Herald of Wales* published a surprising tribute by him in the form of a 32-line poem.

> A woman wails her dead among the trees,
> Under the green roofs grieve the living;
> The living sun laments the dying skies,
> Lamenting falls. Pity Electra's loving.

But his fellow theatre members could also find Dylan as tiresome as had his former employers. In a production of a Spanish romance, one leading light, Elizabeth Iorwerth, was playing the part of a young society girl who was giving up the world and love to join a nunnery. At its most touching moment, the young actress giving her all, there was a loud disturbance at the back of the hall. When she asked what had caused it, the answer was 'Oh that awful Dylan Thomas, he came in late and was pretending to be sick'. She had the wit to say that it wasn't an unreasonable reaction.

Sometimes he failed to turn up to rehearsals, only to be word perfect with flawless diction on the night, or nipped off to the local pub, known as Cheese's (because the landlord was a Mr Cheddar). The pub and the hall were connected by a flight of steps and close enough for a character who was not on stage to belt down and warn a fellow performer that they were about to go on. Dylan was by now so used to getting away with bad behaviour that on one occasion he defied a producer who told him close to the opening night that if he went for a quick one, he needn't come back. He didn't. Soon after, Ethel Ross was sitting at the back of the auditorium watching the dress rehearsal, with a replacement playing his part, when he slipped in and sat down next to her like a little boy. The producer was down at the front. 'She's a nasty wicked woman and I don't love her,' Dylan whispered. He had taken great umbrage, and his subsequent appearances on the Little Theatre stage were few and far between.

Charles Fisher by Alfred Janes, 1937. A school friend of
Janes and Thomas, who also worked with the poet
on the Swansea Daily Post

CHAPTER THREE

GOING FREELANCE

Cut adrift from his anchors at the *Evening Post* and the Little Theatre, Dylan's social life revolved around the Kardomah and his friends' houses. Charlie was still at the paper and thanks to an indulgent chief reporter, spent a lot of time at the cafe. Its premises were in an old Congregational chapel (where D.J. and Florence had married). Respectable types sat on the ground floor, but Charlie, Dylan and their friends sat upstairs to drink coffee – not the real thing but Camp coffee, made mostly of chicory essence, topped up with hot water and a dash of milk, which at tuppence ha'penny (2½d) was all they could afford. Here the so-called 'Kardomah Gang' traded news and conversation, something that they were all good at. Dylan captured the spirit in his nostalgic 1947 broadcast, *Return Journey*, in which the narrator revisits the town of his youth and asks after 'Young Thomas':

Passer By:
Oh, him! He owes me half a crown. I haven't seen him since the old Kardomah Days. He wasn't a reporter then, he'd just left the grammar school. Him and Charlie Fisher – Charlie's got whiskers now – and Tom Warner and Fred Janes, drinking coffee dashes and arguing the toss.

Narrator:
What about?

Passer By:
*Music and poetry and painting and politics. Einstein and Epstein,
Stravinsky and Greta Garbo, death and religion, Picasso and girls...*

Narrator:
And then?

Passer By:
*Communism, symbolism, Bradman, Braque, the Watch Committee,
free love, free beer, murder, Michelangelo, ping-pong, ambition, Sibelius
and girls...*

Narrator:
Is that all?

Passer By:
*How Dan Jones was going to compose the most prodigious symphony,
Fred Janes paint the most miraculously meticulous picture, Charlie
Fisher catch the poshest trout, Vernon Watkins and Young Thomas
write the most boiling poems, how they would ring the bells of London
and paint it like a tart...*

Narrator:
And after that?

Passer By:
*Oh the hissing of the butt-ends in the drains of the coffee-dashes and
the tinkle and gibble-gabble of the morning young lounge lizards as
they talked about Augustus John, Emil Jannings, Carnera, Dracula,
Amy Johnson, trial marriage, pocket money, the Welsh sea, the
London stars, King Kong, anarchy, darts, T.S. Eliot, and girls...*

In fact both Charlie and Fred agreed that there was no such thing as a Kardomah group in the sense of a collection of people who shared commonly held artistic or social aims. Dan and the poet Vernon Watkins did not even meet until the 1940s. They might have realised that there was an outstanding poet in their midst, but they were all too interested in themselves to show any deference to Dylan. Neither were they particularly tightly knit. Dylan was making the first of many visits up to London; Fred and Mervyn Levy were living there during term time and from 1935 Dan too. His family had moved to Harrow and after graduating from Swansea University, he won a place at the Royal Academy of Music where he studied conducting with Sir Henry Wood, composition, viola and horn. Dylan and Fred's weekend visits to stay with Dan's family were a welcome retreat from the squalor of Earls Court, where the exiled Uplands Bohemians carried on exactly as they had at home. But in 1936 he won a prestigious travelling Mendelssohn scholarship for young musicians that took him around Europe. Those who were still in Swansea, like Charlie, were all ears: 'We paid rapt attention to Dylan's stories of adventures in the great City, his first meetings with the famous, Surrealism and the Sitwells.'

The musical soirées continued at Tom Warner's house with the usual collection of 'instruments', and there would be parties and parlour games at friends' houses. Charades with a literary bent were a favourite – Fred recalled dressing up with Dan in workman-like clothes, rolling up a couple of mats and carrying them out of the room to act out the title of Dostoyevsky's *The Brothers Karamazov*. Dylan's ability to use a few props and put on accents to create a character was so entertaining that charades often turned into a one-man show: Harpo Marx, his favourite brother in the films that he adored, was a personal triumph.

The home of the Phillips sisters Vera and Evelyn, or 'Titch', was particularly welcoming – their brother had been taught by D.J. at the grammar school. The family also had a beach hut at Langland Bay, the nearest desirable seaside village on the Gower coast and 'the Mentone [sic] of Wales' according to an advertisement for the Langland Bay Hotel, a popular venue for five-shilling Saturday night dinner dances. One friend of Charlie's, on asking his father what he should put down as his religion on a form he was filling in, got the reply: 'Better put down the Langland Bay Hotel'.

Dylan had met the Phillips girls on a camping trip to Gower when he was still a schoolboy. Titch was struck by this 'little shrimp of a boy with light curly hair' and his 'remarkable voice'.

He read her some of his poems, which she confessed she found hard to understand, but was very impressed when he explained to her the meaning of 'idiosyncrasy', a word she had come across at school. Camping in Rhossili, the village at the western tip of the peninsula where majestic Worm's Head flanks the huge expanse of sandy beach, was a regular fixture. While Dylan's survival skills were negligible – he was cut off by the tide more than once on Worm's Head – he could hold a bunch of schoolboys spellbound with stories around the campfire.

Dylan also impressed his companions with his terrier-like determination not to be defeated in a fight, even by boys twice his size. 'He wouldn't give in. If he thought he was being beaten, he'd still fight on,' one friend observed. In a short story called 'Extraordinary Little Cough', a lad given that nickname who is bullied by bigger boys proves that he can run five miles along the length of Rhossili beach and back. 'I ran every bit of it! You said I couldn't and I did! I've been running and running!' he exclaims triumphantly. As Charlie Fisher pointed out, Dylan's puny looks belied stamina that was, indeed, extraordinary.

Dylan also invited friends to Cwmdonkin Drive, where Fred, Tom and Charlie would 'talk and laugh our heads off' when he was back from London. Florence kept them going with 'tables of sandwiches', tea and Welshcakes, and if they had been to the pub, sometimes Dylan stopped at Fred's sister's house to sober up before he headed home. Kitty Janes had shocked her chapel-going parents by eloping at eighteen with a local car mechanic in his red Bugatti. Fred painted his older sibling in a splendidly vampish pose in 1932 as a piece of RA 'homework', but their mother was furious because in the picture Kitty is languidly holding a cigarette, although she didn't smoke. When Mrs Janes demanded of her son why he had done this, he replied: 'Because I wanted to'. Now he was lodging with the young couple in the Uplands, just down the hill from Cwmdonkin Drive. Kitty sometimes typed Dylan's poems for him, and as a very young housewife with a baby daughter, looked forward to the young man's visits, which were always good fun, even if Dylan's antics included eating the flowers in her vases.

At Cwmdonkin Drive, Dylan read aloud the latest poems in his notebooks, or sometimes written on the back of large sheets of card that kept shirts flat when they came back from the laundry. 'We were spellbound with the richness of his voice and his quite uncanny power of bringing clarity to verse that seemed so obscure in print,' Fred recalled. 'It seems to me that at this time he brought to its full development his most personal and dynamic way of reading, which was to make him a much-sought-after broadcaster and speaker.'

Fred also met Dylan's new friend: 'Bert Trick, grocer and man of letters'. Outside Dylan's usual circle and sixteen years his senior, Bert came from a prosperous local family of meat traders, whose business had faltered in the deep recession of the 1930s. While Dylan's friends were firmly rooted in Swansea's bourgeoisie and fairly immune to the effects of the 'great slump' on working-class people, they could not ignore its impact. His story 'Just Like Little Dogs' evokes the bleak, hopeless world of young men with nothing

51

to do but stand under the railway arches smoking. The families of miners, dockers and factory workers in the Swansea valley were hit hard as unemployment rose, and there were plenty of men hanging around the town's streets in threadbare suits, mufflers and cloth caps, barely surviving on inadequate dole money. The British Union of Fascists had opened an office near the Uplands in 1931. Walking past it one evening, Fred and Dylan overheard two young men deciding to join up for want of anything else to do. Sir Oswald Mosley recognised the recruitment potential and addressed a rally at the Plaza cinema, the largest in Wales, in 1934. It ended in uproar after a vicar in the audience asked Mosley if, given that he worked for a Jew, he should change his employer and the fascist leader answered yes. Dylan was there and wrote to a local paper afterwards in outraged protest.

Bert had tried to turn around his fortunes by opening a grocery store in the Uplands, but this also failed to prosper and he joined the Labour Party, expressing his increasingly left-wing views in contributions to local papers and forming a group to discuss politics, music and art. Dylan was introduced to him by one of the producers at the Little Theatre, a university English lecturer called Thomas Taig, who had written a book on rhythm and metre and encouraged the young poet to show Bert his work. Dylan called on the grocer one evening with a sheaf of poems, which he insisted on reading aloud.

Like Fred, Bert and his wife were spellbound by his rich voice and delivery. The young poet and the radical grocer became close friends, sharing their passion for words. 'There was no need for strong drink, we were intoxicated with words – ideas and words,' Trick wrote later. Dylan's reward for Bert's delight in his poetry was to discuss politics, philosophy and religion with an older, wiser man who was to help him mature as a writer. Poems like 'The hunchback in the park' revealed Dylan's genuine compassion for the dispossessed, and his early notebook poems showed how the teenager wrestled with a quasi-religious conflict between life and death, flesh and spirit. Bert was able to put some intellectual meat on the bones of Dylan's mental maelstrom, and the boy who had tackled bigger bullies and rebelled against authority at school began to grasp an ideological framework for his sense of man's place in the world – if a rather shaky one. Poetry would always be a more potent calling than politics for Dylan.

Bert was also responsible for a turning point on Dylan's chosen path of becoming a freelance writer and poet. He had been encouraging his protégé to submit poems to London literary magazines for publication and in May 1933, 'And death shall have no dominion' was accepted by a fledgling periodical, *New English Weekly*. Dylan was not yet twenty, but its timeless theme and powerful imagery made it one of his most loved and enduring pieces.

And death shall have no dominion.
Dead man naked they shall be one
With the man in the wind and the west moon;
When their bones are picked clean and the clean bones gone,
They shall have stars at elbow and foot;

Though they go mad they shall be sane,
Though they sink through the sea they shall rise again;
Though lovers be lost love shall not;
And death shall have no dominion...

May 1933 brought another watershed. Life at Cwmdonkin Drive was becoming intolerable for Nancy. D.J. was increasingly maudlin, often thanks to drink, and worried about money – perhaps not surprisingly with two unemployed children under his roof. Haydn had got a job in London and Nancy's letters to him described D.J.'s foul-mouthed, often physical attacks on her and claimed that Dylan was stealing from her purse to feed his increasingly regular habit of coming home drunk. She finally escaped by marrying Haydn that month and moving to Surrey. This gave Dylan a pretext for visiting his Swansea friends in London and developing another of his natural talents: finding a bed for the night. Encouraged by his success with the *New English Weekly*, despite the lack of a fee, he made his first visit in the summer of 1933, staying with a much older Swansea Grammar School friend and forming another lifelong habit – drinking at the Fitzroy Tavern off Tottenham Court Road. Dylan's ability to stand out from the crowd also began to emerge – in June another poem, 'The romantic isle', was selected as an entry for a BBC poetry competition and read on air. In September, after Dylan had met its editor at Bert's suggestion, *Adelphi* published another poem, 'No man believes, when a star falls shot'. This time it was paid for. Momentum was building.

Back in Swansea, Dylan was as keen to escape the atmosphere in Cwmdonkin Drive as Nancy. To make matters worse, D.J. had been diagnosed with cancer of the tongue. Dylan took refuge with Florence's relations on the Llansteffan peninsula in the lush, low hills of south Carmarthenshire, where he had spent school holidays on his Aunt Ann and Uncle Jim's small-holding, Fernhill. It was a complete antidote to the confines of Cwmdonkin Drive, which Dylan recreated in his story 'The Peaches', renaming Fernhill 'Gorsehill', a ramshackle collection of buildings around a yard where 'a bucketful of old bedraggled hens scratched and laid small eggs' and Ann kept pigs and cows, whose milk she churned into butter to sell. Here Dylan the schoolboy had chased rabbits or played Indians in the Gorsehill jungle swarming, the violent, impossible birds and fishes leaping ... I felt all my young body like an excited animal surrounding me, the torn knees bent, the bumping heart, the long heat and depth between the legs, the sweat prickling in the hands ... I was aware of myself in the exact middle of a living story.

Aunt Ann would 'fuss and cluck' over him, making hot broth and potatoes, tea and mustard baths to keep him warm inside the dark, damp house, molly-coddling him in the way his mother did. But a stranger side of life in remote, chapel-going west Wales surfaces in his cousin, 'Gwilym' in the story, who is training to be a preacher and invites Dylan to attend mock services in the barn, with its 'bat-lined rafters and hanging webs'. Drunken sinner Uncle Jim sells the animals Aunt Ann has raised and spends the proceeds in the pub. 'Last Christmas he took a sheep over his shoulder, and he was pissed for ten days,' Gwilym reports. Dylan would make many more visits to the area as he grew up, and the childhood memories of Fernhill would be distilled more purely into one of his most evocative and moving poems – 'Fern Hill'. But 'The Peaches', with its visceral connection to the natural world of west Wales and fondness for the simple warmth of its people, coupled with an awareness of its darker undercurrents and influences, has all the ingredients of a work that was to make Dylan world famous – *Under Milk Wood*. He made many more visits to the area as he grew up, but probably did not visit the little town most closely associated with the play, and where he spent some of the happiest days of his life, until the following year.

Dylan set off for Llansteffan again on the Whitsun weekend of 1934. This time he was with another connection in his growing literary network, Glyn Jones, a young writer and teacher who contacted Dylan after reading one of his poems in the *Adelphi*.

Glyn also had roots in the Llansteffan area and the two decided to drive down in his car, then take the rowing-boat ferry in a 'hell-mouthed mist' across the river Taf to Laugharne on the opposite side where they strolled around the town, visited the parish church and took tea in Brown's Hotel. If Dylan had visited 'the strangest town in Wales' before, with its castle, town hall and population of 400 governed by a 700-year-old corporation headed by a portreeve, this was the first time it made an impression on him. He described it in a letter to Pamela Hansford Johnson:

> I can never do justice … to the miles and miles and miles of mud and grey sand, to the un-nerving silence of the fisherwomen, & the mean-souled cries of the gulls & the herons, to the shapes of the fisherwomen's breasts that drop, big as barrels, over the stained tops of their overalls as they bend over the sand, to the cows in the fields that lie north of the sea…

If the tone sounds bleak, Dylan soon cheered up when the sun came out and at the thought that 'The Three Mariners will have undone their waistcoats. I shall drink beer with the portreeve, and no crimping pussyfoot will say me nay.' The next time Dylan visited Laugharne would be in 1936, in pursuit of a different girlfriend. His letter to Pamela was full of repressed sexual longing and anxiety about death – perhaps reflecting his father's ill health and the worries it prompted about the effects of his own drinking and smoking. In his next letter to her, he confessed that on his way back to Swansea from Laugharne he had stayed with a friend in Gower and, after one too many at the pub, been seduced by his friend's fiancée, with whom – he said – he spent the following three nights in bed. It was the beginning of the end of his long-distance and unconsummated romance with Pamela. They had seriously considered getting married, but Dylan's infidelities apart, it was his relationship with alcohol that worried Pamela, and the affair ended. She later married the chemist and novelist C. P. Snow, who famously wrote about the breakdown in communication between science and the humanities in his lecture 'The Two Cultures'. It would take a less cultured Irishwoman to match Dylan's thirst for beer.

Vernon Watkins by Alfred Janes, 1946

CHAPTER FOUR

SWANSEA'S OTHER POET

Back in Cwmdonkin Drive, Dylan was working extremely hard. In the two years between leaving the *Post* and moving up to London to live with Fred in 1934, he had filled notebooks with more than 200 poems. He would draw on these for *18 Poems* when it was published in December that year, as well as writing five new ones in October for inclusion. When the book was prominently displayed in the window of a Swansea bookshop early in 1935, it came as a shock to a man who was eight years older and thought he was the only bard in town. Vernon Watkins, a young bank clerk who filled in ledgers by day but wrote poetry in the evenings and at weekends, was somewhat put out to discover there was another one. Although he bought and admired Dylan's collection, he made no attempt to meet him until he bumped into Dylan's uncle, the preacher at Paraclete Chapel in Mumbles, which Vernon had attended as a child. His parents were chapelgoers and close friends of the Reverend Rees and his wife.

The Reverend Dai Rees was Florence's brother-in-law. Dylan stayed with him and his Aunt Dosie at the manse belonging to Paraclete, where he worshipped on Sundays with his mother – or so his mother liked to think. But Dylan came to detest the bible-thumping, hellfire-and-brimstone style of Welsh preaching, with its sing-song cadence and crescendoing emotional fervour known as 'hwyl'. A notebook poem about 'The Reverend Crap, a pious fraud', has 'Rev. David Rees' scrawled above it. The minister didn't have much time for modern poetry either, and is said to have told Florence that Dylan was mad and should be locked up. Dylan's response was to write a poem which began 'I hate you from your dandruff to your corns'.

When Vernon bumped into Rees, he suggested that he should look up his nephew and gave him the Thomases' address in Cwmdonkin Drive. Dylan was out when Vernon called but telephoned him the next day and was invited to his family's home, Heatherslade, named after a nearby cove at Pennard, just along the Gower coast from beautiful Three Cliffs Bay. Vernon remembered the meeting very clearly: 'He was rather shy, but intense and eager in manner, deep-voiced, restless, very humorous, with large, wondering eyes and under those the face of a cherub.' They went for a walk along the cliff tops, which here drop down steeply and are peppered with gorse bushes and sheep paths leading down to rocky coves. But the views across to Three Cliffs and the sandy sweep of Oxwich Bay are among the most spectacular on the British coast. Back at the Watkins family home, Dylan heard Vernon read a few of his poems and was amused when he asked to see more and Vernon produced a whole trunkful. Vernon appreciated immediately that Dylan was a very constructive critic, who could quickly tell 'what was fresh in my work and what was not'.

It was the beginning of one of the most significant friendships of Dylan's life, and probably the most meaningful of Vernon's, despite their age gap and very different backgrounds. Vernon's family were well-to-do; his father, as Vernon later joked, was the youngest manager of Lloyds Bank in Swansea, while Vernon was its oldest clerk. Mrs Watkins was from a minor county family in west Wales and Vernon had spent his childhood in Caswell Bay, another of Swansea's des res seaside villages, in a large house right on the beach with a tennis court and billiard room. Mrs Watkins employed a cook, maids and a gardener, but did everything for her son, from tying his shoelaces to pumping up his bicycle tyres. Like Dylan's parents, both she and her husband were Welsh speaking, but did not bring up their children bilingual, making sure that any trace of a Swansea accent in Vernon was eradicated in elocution lessons.

This privileged upbringing, combined with boarding at prep school and then Repton, made it difficult for the unworldly Vernon, his head in a cloud of poems, to stand on his own two feet. Despite winning a place at Cambridge to study modern languages, an independent, academic life did not suit him. 'It was too much criticism and not enough original work,' he later told his wife Gwen. 'No point staying where you have to read inferior people when you could be reading the greats.' He left, working first for Lloyds Bank in Cardiff, then after a breakdown during which he returned to Repton and attacked the headmaster, back in Swansea. Poetry was always Vernon's main love, but until he met Dylan it was a very solitary affair. 'Swansea was not really a place where poetry was tremendously important but it meant a tremendous lot to him,' according to Gwen in her memoir *Dylan Thomas: Portrait of a Friend*. 'There was a lady called Myfanwy Haycock who wrote poems for the *Evening Post* about spring and forgotten ladies, that sort of thing. Later on lots of people used to send Vernon poems to read and sometimes he would say "Oh dear, Myfanwy Haycock"'.

In Dylan he found someone who cared as deeply and passionately as he did. Both thought W.B. Yeats the greatest living poet – though Dylan said Thomas Hardy was his favourite. And both were prepared to spend hours discussing their own work, listening to each other reading aloud and suggesting changes, although Dylan once announced: 'I refute your criticism from the bottom of my catarrh'. The two young poets shared another love:

cricket. Vernon was very sporty, played both tennis and squash and loved swimming off the rocks at Heatherslade. Dylan was more of a spectator and they both enjoyed going to matches at the ground in Swansea – especially if Glamorgan, the county side, was playing.

Dylan soon invited Fred to Cwmdonkin Drive to meet the other poet and they hit it off immediately. Vernon became a close friend and all three began to spend a great deal of time together, as Fred recalled:

> During the years immediately preceding the war, Dylan and I frequently took the bus on Sundays to spend the day with Vernon and his family. They were all extremely gentle, hospitable and cultivated. Dylan's behaviour was invariably impeccable – charming, very funny and altogether lovable. None of them ever believed there was ever any other kind of Dylan.

Vernon quickly became part of the Kardomah circle on Saturday afternoons if he wasn't playing hockey, or during his lunch hour at the bank, when he would join Charlie Fisher, Tom Warner, and Dylan and Fred when they were in town. If no one was to be found in the Kardomah, then Fred's studio nearby was a useful port of call and kind of communications post, where a piece of paper was stuck on the wall for everyone to scribble messages suggesting a time and place to meet. Vernon knew little about modern art, which was definitely not on show in Swansea, and according to Gwen, was staggered by Fred's work. Fred, flattered by the attention, would take Vernon to the studio to show him the latest work in progress, often based on the gorgeous blooms in the family shop. 'The studio, high above a flower shop near Swansea station, could only be reached by climbing a stair which held every variety of smell from the flowers to the pickled objects he painted, fish, fruit and lobsters…' Vernon said. Gwen believes that the Kardomah was 'a kind of nurturing place. They put each other down and were sarcastic, but they all took the arts seriously and it gave them what they couldn't get from their middle-class mums and dads. They all thought that what they were going to do would be *good*.'

Fred in his Swansea studio, c.1935

When *18 Poems* came out that confidence, in Dylan's case, was proved right. Comments in London literary magazines included 'One of the most remarkable books of poetry which has appeared for several years' (*European Quarterly*) and 'I credit Dylan Thomas with being the first considerable poet to break through fashionable limitation and speak an unborrowed language, without excluding anything that preceded him' *(Time and Tide)*.

It would be some time before Vernon saw a published volume

of his copious output, but Fred and Mervyn were both finding favour in London's art world, as Dylan and Charlie's old outlet, the *Swansea Grammar School* magazine, reported in March 1936. Their success seems to have taken their alma mater by surprise. The article, entitled 'Arcades Ambo' (two of a kind), pompous and patronising by turns, begins:

> We are constantly hearing of the success of Old Boys, particularly in the academic spheres, but so far we have had little to report about boys who have taken art as a career. However, there are two Old Boys who have had considerable success in this direction. These two lived and worked together in what might be described as a somewhat Bohemian manner, in London, sharing their rooms for several years with yet another Old Boy, Dylan Thomas, who has made a name for himself in the realm of modern poetry. These two artists are Alfred Janes and Mervyn Levy.

It goes on to list the many prizes and scholarships won by Fred and Mervyn at the RA and the RCA, and notes proudly that Fred's portrait of Dylan had been 'considered good enough, when exhibited in Swansea and Cardiff in the recent Exhibition of Welsh Art, to be purchased by the National Museum of Wales'. It also records that both old boys held one-man shows in the foyer of the Everyman Cinema at Hampstead. Mervyn definitely sounds a little 'advanced', rejecting the prevailing Modernist trends in art:

> Levy's work is quite unconventional. He feels that he can express himself best in the manner we associate with Eastern Races, and confesses to being deeply influenced by Indian Art. We are given to understand by those capable of judging that

he has the ability to go a long way as a draughtsman and painter, and that when his work is a little more mature it will deserve wider recognition.

Keen to capitalise on the success of *18 Poems*, Dylan produced another volume less than two years later, this time brokered by an agent, David Higham, and with a major publishing house – Dent. *Twenty-Five Poems* revealed some new work, but mainly he raided his notebooks again, including 'Death shall have no dominion' and 'The hand that signed the paper' – thought of as his only overtly political poem, in that it is about the power of a handful of men to control the life and death of others in a treaty.

A goose's quill has put end to murder
That put an end to talk.

It received mixed reviews, but one accolade was game changing. Dylan first read it on one of his Sunday outings with Fred to visit the Watkins family in Pennard – it was quite a day, Fred recalled. The review was by Edith Sitwell in that day's *Sunday Times*. Edith and her two brothers, Osbert and Sacheverell, were members of a wealthy family and influential members of London's literati. They wrote and published their own work, but also promoted young writers whom they thought promising. Approval from the eccentric and forceful Edith, with her heavily jewelled fingers, bizarre black topknot crowning hooded eyes and a beaked nose, carried enormous weight in London's publishing circles.

'The work of this very young man (he is twenty-two years of age) is on a huge scale, both in theme and structurally,' she wrote. 'I could not name one poet of this, the youngest generation, who shows so great a promise, and even so great an achievement.' The review prompted a furious argument in the paper's letters pages about the nature of modern poetry. 'It was my privilege and pride to give the attackers, during two months, more than as good as they gave,' Edith wrote in her autobiography, *Taken Care Of*. 'The air still seems to reverberate with the sound of numskulls [*sic*] soundly hit.' The debate helped to trigger several reprints of *Twenty-Five Poems*. Edith had been aware of Dylan's work for some time and now she invited him for lunch. It was the start of a long and sincere friendship. 'I have never known anyone so capable of endearing himself to others,' Edith effused. 'And this was not only the result of his great warmth, charm and touching funniness. I have never known anyone with a more holy and childlike innocence of mind ... He loved humanity and had contempt only for the cruel, the unkind ... and the mean.'

These personal qualities were helping Dylan to become what would be described today as a very good networker. His coming and goings at the London digs he had shared with his Swansea friends were explained, Fred realised, by the fact that he was using them as a base to meet people who would either publish his own work or his reviews of other people's. As a young freelance poet from south Wales, this was essential. Now, as Dylan made the 400-mile round trip by rail between Swansea and London, sleeping wherever he could find a bed for the night, his network of friends and supporters grew to include writers like Norman Cameron and Rayner Heppenstall, who were to become valuable contacts at the BBC; editors and influencers like the Sitwells and T.S. Eliot, director at foremost poetry publishers Faber & Faber; Cecil Day Lewis, a future Poet Laureate; and the historian A. J. P. Taylor. His behaviour charmed, dazzled and appalled them by turn, especially if he drank too much. But it was easy to forgive Dylan; Geoffrey Grigson, an influential poet and journal editor, put it nicely: 'When he disappeared, it was a relief; when he reappeared, a pleasure.'

Vernon was one of the first close friends to get wind of the self-destructive nature of Dylan's drinking. He had only seen his fellow poet drunk once before, when they had celebrated Dylan's twenty-second birthday on 27 October 1936 at one of his favourite Mumbles pubs, the Mermaid. (Vernon recorded it much later in a poem called 'Sailors on the Moving Land'.) The inevitable dressing down Dylan got from D.J. on arriving home sloshed at Cwmdonkin Drive was one thing, but upsetting his hosts on the literary circuit was self-defeating, as Wyn Lewis, Vernon's neighbour in Pennard and a childhood friend of Dylan's from the Cwmdonkin Park days, discovered.

Wyn was now reading English at Cambridge and arranged for Dylan to talk to the university's Literary Society. His detailed account is given by Gwen Watkins in her memoir, and what happened followed a pattern that was to repeat itself over and over again in academic circles. Dylan turned up claiming he had already drunk thirty pints of beer – certainly an exaggeration, as he was pleasantly mellow and charming over tea with Wyn and his undergraduate friends. The more formal drinks reception that followed filled Dylan with dread and he had to be physically manhandled there by Wyn and the secretary of the Literary Society, Ian Watt. The hush that fell as he entered the room sent him straight for the sherry, of which he downed several glasses, then he demanded whisky, and with the alcohol rushing to his head, treated the assembled Cambridge dons and their wives to his lecherous Harpo Marx routine – hilarious backstage at the Little Theatre or a Soho pub, but totally inappropriate here.

His behaviour on the journey to the talk at St John's College was just as bad, and when they arrived fifteen minutes late there were only a handful of people in the room – the horrified reception guests had decided to boycott Dylan's performance. Passers-by were dragged in from the street and after a faltering start, his 'wild, brilliant and anarchic' twenty-page, handwritten lecture on contemporary literature prompted so much laughter that more people kept coming in to see what all the fuss was about. It ended in rapturous applause with the adoring audience crowding around him. It was probably the first example of the unease and insecurity a young man who had failed academically and left school at sixteen felt in the company of academics. His coping mechanism was to drink to lose his inhibitions and then win his audience around with a bravura performance.

The wandering minstrel's lifestyle was beginning to take its toll on Dylan's wellbeing. Hobnobbing in literary London slowed his output down, as the contents of the mainly notebook-based collection in *Twenty-Five Poems* showed. And Dylan was paying the price for his encounters with the seedier side of Bohemian life. As well as his persistent cough, the poor nutrition of his liquid diet and its resulting hangovers, he had reportedly picked up a dose of gonorrhoea, for which he blamed, colourfully, a 'chorus girl with glasses' called Fluffy. The treatment – washing out the urethra with water (antibiotics were not available in the 1930s) – sent him scuttling back to Cwmdonkin Drive. His mother, on being asked by a neighbour what was wrong, said she didn't know, 'but every time he goes to the lavatory he screams'. At twenty-two years old, the script for Dylan's life was already written. It was a tale of triumphs and disasters: despite a dismal school career, he had a profound understanding of English literature, but no time for pompous or pretentious academics. He couldn't hold down an office job, but had demonstrated his natural ability to act and entertain an audience. He had a group of very close friends from his hometown, who supported him in his deep need and utter determination to write poetry, and an ever-expanding network of powerful literary patrons who appreciated his mischievous wit, charm and talent. But his provincial would-be Bohemian tastes for beer, cigarettes and the wrong sort of women could easily drive him off course; and his adoring mother – with the best of intentions – had inadvertently nurtured a son who was incapable of looking after himself. But in this year, 1936, he met someone who would profoundly affect how this story would unfold: Caitlin Macnamara.

Caitlin Macnmara, Dylan's future wife, posing as a dancer
on the banks of the river Avon in Hampshire
for Nora Summers

CHAPTER FIVE

THE FAIRY PRINCESS

'Dylan told me that I was beautiful, that he loved me and that he was going to marry me, and he kept on repeating these phrases as though he had at last found the girl who was right for him and we were meant for each other.' That was Caitlin's account of their first meeting in the spring of 1936 in her third memoir about their lives together. It was co-written when she was in her seventies, so her recall of events may not have been accurate, and in any case Caitlin's memory did not always serve her well. But whether he said it or not that evening in the Wheatsheaf pub in Fitzrovia, it was all true. Dylan did fall deeply in love with 22-year-old Caitlin; she was beautiful and they did get married. It is also true that Caitlin was a woman who desperately craved love, attention and admiration.

Her background could not have been more different to Dylan's. If he and his suburban arty friends pretended to be Bohemians, Caitlin was the real deal. 'We were all predestined victims for alcoholism and decadence because we had nothing to hold us,' is how she described the way she and her two sisters and brother were brought up. Today the Macnamaras would be labelled as a dysfunctional family. Francis, her father, was a member of the Irish gentry who fancied himself as a philosopher and man of letters. The family home was a mansion in Ennistymon in Co. Clare, but Francis moved to Dublin, where he lived opposite W.B. Yeats and went to the poet's literary soirées. Dylan and Vernon would have been wild with envy at her meeting their greatest living poet but Caitlin just found Yeats 'appallingly pretentious'.

Francis was a hopeless parent. 'I suppose Francis could have been called a womaniser, although I don't think he was what I would call a real womaniser,' she wrote in her memoir *Caitlin: A Warring Absence*. Her reasoning indicates just how wobbly her moral compass was, even with sixty years' perspective. 'He did have three wives, affairs with other women and an illegitimate daughter by a woman who worked as a nurse in a mental home, but he didn't seem able to treat his women very well.' Francis and their mother, Yvonne, separated when she was eight. Caitlin resented his neglect of his children and had little contact with him. The last time she saw him was in her late teens in Blashford, Hampshire, where Yvonne had gone to live near the leading portrait painter of the day, Pembrokeshire-born Augustus John. An infamously eccentric figure, he had become a family friend on his travels around Ireland in a gypsy caravan, his wife, mistress and several children in tow.

At Blashford Yvonne met a rich artist friend of John's, Nora Summers, to whom she became very attached. 'Sometimes in the afternoons they would disappear into my mother's bedroom and lock the door behind them, so it was pretty obvious what was going on,' said Caitlin. The 'odious' Nora became another cause of resentment and self-pity. 'We children looked upon her as an absolute monster who had taken our mother from us. Nora was the father figure of our childhood, and an evil one.' Yvonne, an elegant woman, who had been brought up in some style by her French mother, treated her children as if they, too, were rich, and expected the lovely Caitlin, with her lustrous blond curls, big blue eyes and petite, curvaceous figure, to marry well. She was horrified when she found out that Caitlin was madly in love with John's son Caspar. John had nine children – that he acknowledged, at least –

and Caspar was one of seven boys. A future First Sea Lord, 'he was tall dark and handsome … unbelievably good looking, with a voice that was low and enchanting'.

The Macnamaras would often dine at the Johns' home at Fryern Court, where guests included eminent philosophers and writers like Bertrand Russell, Lord David Cecil and T. E. Lawrence. John loved to hold court and expound his theories about Romany culture and the gypsies being descendants of primitive man, which Caitlin found boring and ridiculous. The part of the soirées she enjoyed most were pre-dinner drinks on the sofa with Caspar and his brother and sisters. Later, she said she and Caspar would sometimes sneak off for secret midnight picnics on the Downs, where they rolled around on the grass kissing and hugging. Eventually Caitlin got Caspar into bed and while she 'wanted him passionately' he didn't respond – which only made her want him more.

When he finally cut her dead one day at Nora's house she was distraught. Although she wrote to him she never got an explanation – until years later when her sister told her that Yvonne had told Caspar to break things off because, as he was ten years her senior, she thought him too old for her daughter. Caitlin's first teenage love affair ended in rejection and despair. With little to distract her apart from riding in the New Forest and hunting for birds' nests with the John children, Caitlin was as bored at home as at the boarding school to which she had been dispatched. She fantasised about becoming a glamorous ballet dancer, acting out her dreams with pliés in her bedroom. After pestering her mother for two years, she was finally allowed to go to London with Vivien John, Caspar's sister, to study tap and acrobatic dance. It was not what Caitlin, who saw herself as prima ballerina material, had in mind, but she loved it all the same.

Her good looks and lovely figure, now honed by practising back walkovers and cartwheels, did not go unnoticed by Augustus John, who invited her to his London studio to model for him. In her memoir she describes how the sitting took place in total silence with John, now in his forties, black haired and bearded, staring at her fiercely. When he had finished, he raped her. 'He suddenly leapt on me, pulling up my dress and tearing off my pants, and made love to me, although you could hardly call it love. It was totally unexpected and I was still a virgin ... I couldn't resist because he was an enormous, strong bestial man. I was cowed and too frightened to resist.' Afterwards John adjusted his clothes and left the room without a word, according to Caitlin.

Despite her romps with Caspar she was completely ignorant about sex – her mother had not even explained what periods are – and felt both repelled and fascinated by this first experience of it. When she went back the next day – 'I had to – the painting wasn't finished' – the same thing happened again. John painted several highly romanticised portraits of Caitlin, and every time she sat, she knew what would happen next. 'It was horrible, with his great hairy face: I don't know why I didn't fight it; why I just let him get on with it when I certainly had no pleasure myself. It was like being attacked by a goat.'

One reason she put up with it, she admitted, was because he took her out for lunches and dinners at fashionable restaurants, introducing her as Francis's daughter. They would stay the night at his flat in Fitzroy Square, which Caitlin saw as 'a necessary sacrifice'. Most – male – biographers are sceptical about Caitlin's credibility, pointing out that she was a coquettish flirt, but to 21st-century ears, this sounds like a story of a powerful, predatory sexual abuser who exploited a vulnerable young family friend by providing the attention and glamour that she craved. When John introduced Caitlin to his drinking pal Dylan Thomas in a Fitzrovia pub in spring 1936, Dylan may well have found her highly attractive, as most men did, but he had no concept of the emotional baggage she was carrying. 'The saddest thing,' Caitlin concluded in *A Warring Absence*, 'is that my whole sexual development happened the wrong way round. It was a catastrophe from which I have never quite recovered'.

The young poet's challenge to the older artist's hold over Caitlin produced some farcical results. That summer, Fred had entered five paintings in a competition at the National Eisteddfod, being held in Fishguard, Pembrokeshire. The exhibition was to be hung by Augustus John and Fred decided to borrow his father's car to drive down there from Swansea to hear the results. Dylan, having recovered from his apparent bout of gonorrhoea, offered to accompany him. He knew that John and Caitlin were staying in Laugharne with Richard Hughes, a writer, and used the pretext of meeting him to make the short detour to see Caitlin. Hughes was the author of *A High Wind in Jamaica*, a popular pirate adventure story, and lived in a handsome Georgian house next to ruined Laugharne castle. After lunch the party set off for Fishguard, stopping off at several pubs on the way, and again on the way back. It was a disappointing outing for Fred – he did not win a prize. John had selected only two of his works to show. 'I don't think he likes my work – he did once, very much – he persuaded Cardiff to buy Dylan and the pink fish but I couldn't stop developing because of that, could I?' Fred commented, adding, tartly: 'After all, I'm not a John fan'.

On the way back to Laugharne his car broke down. Dylan got into the back seat of John's car with Caitlin, where they started canoodling, watched in the rear view mirror by their outraged driver. Another pub stop followed and before Dylan could get back in the car John knocked him to the ground and drove off to Laugharne with Caitlin at high speed. Dylan had to make his way home on public transport. But nothing, for now, was going to come between the couple. In October that year Dylan wrote a passionate love letter to Caitlin.

> I love you: it's almost too wonderful (to me) to say, but I want to say it and I want to say it and I am saying it – I love you; and we'll always keep each other alive. We can never do nothing at all now but that both of us know about it. You can do anything & be anything as long as it's with me. This, as you might gather Miss Macnamara, is from Dylan – & God, he must be with you soon.

Nine months later, Vernon received a letter from Dylan saying that he and Caitlin had married.

> My own news is very big and simple. I was married three days ago, to Caitlin Macnamara; in Penzance register office; with no money, no prospect of money, no attendant friends or relatives, and in complete happiness … I think you'll like [her] very much, she looks like the princess on the top of a Christmas tree, or like a stage Wendy; but, for God's sake, don't tell her that.

Dylan had visited Cornwall for the first time the year before, and returned with Caitlin to stay at a friend's cottage in remote and dramatic Lamorna Cove. He had written to his parents about their marriage plans, but D.J. and Florence were dead against it and even persuaded their son-in-law, Haydn, to phone Yvonne Macnamara in an attempt to put a stop to it. D.J. finally faced the inevitable and sent them some money, but even so a friend had to put them up and pay for the ceremony, the money they had stashed away to pay for the licence having been spent. Without an income or a roof over their heads, the newlyweds were dependent on friends and family. The next year or so was spent staying with Caitlin's mother in Hampshire, where Nora Summers had seemingly been forgiven enough to take some of the most iconic photographs of Dylan and his young wife, or back in Swansea with the Thomases. They had moved to a village on the outskirts of Gower, where Dylan surprised Caitlin with his impeccable behaviour once back in the family home, but she was shocked at how Florence mothered him. 'She had coddled him so much that he didn't even know how to take the top off an egg.'

Caitlin Macnamara photographed by Nora Summers in the summer of 1936 by the river Avon near her home in Hampshire

Dylan also took her to Vernon's home in Pennard, where she learned to play croquet and enjoyed scampering down the cliffs to swim off the rocks. The Watkinses, like all Dylan's Swansea friends, were struck by Caitlin's beauty. Ethel Ross, on her way to the Little Theatre one lovely evening, saw them at the bus stop, though they didn't notice her. 'The girl was brighter than the evening, fair curly hair, intensely blue eyes, fresh complexion, bright lips, all smiles, dancing up and down the curb in little white kid boots.' Ethel didn't know it at the time, but Dylan was taking his new bride to meet his parents.

There were occasional essential forays to London in search of work, to give readings and attend events on the avant-garde art scene, of which Dylan was now considered a member. The previous year he and Dan Jones had seen the landmark International Surrealist Exhibition. It was attended by thousands of visitors and eminent thinkers gave lectures. Salvador Dalí delivered his in a diving outfit and nearly suffocated. Dan and Dylan delighted in the tea set lined with squirrel fur and adjusted the mobiles hanging from the ceiling when they thought no one was looking.

Despite this peripatetic lifestyle, Dylan was writing poems and short stories, which he often sent to Vernon to type up and for comments. He also encouraged Vernon to send his own, hitherto unpublished, verse to a new Welsh literary magazine, which accepted two of his pieces. But the normally forgiving Vernon was infuriated when he realised that Dylan had rewritten parts of them and he altered by hand every copy he could find in Swansea's bookshops. Dylan also upset his agent, David Higham, by dealing behind his back with publishers – another worrying example of his scant regard for (or at least ignorance of) the rules of publishing conduct. It was partly a sign of desperation. Unlike Vernon, who had his steady job at the bank and was happy to live with his parents in Pennard, Dylan and Caitlin were penniless. When a new American publishing house, New Directions, started taking an interest in his work, Dylan rashly and probably somewhat naively tried to make deals behind his agent's back.

Fred had found it hard to make his way too, and had returned permanently to Swansea after his spell among the writers and artists of St Ives in Cornwall, partly to support his mother after the death of his father in late 1936. The geometric grids that had begun to appear on his portraits of Dylan and Mervyn were now becoming very complex, often inspired by his love of music and

78

Dan's explanations of its formal structures. Just as a composer would take a musical motif or theme and play with it in a piece of music, Fred took a detailed motif from the main subject of his still life – a bowl of hyacinths, a lobster, a kipper and pineapple – and use it as a repeat pattern for a drape or tablecloth, or the background of the painting. Incising the complex grid with a penknife when he had finished, and softening the mark with turpentine gave them their jewel-like quality. In 1937 he produced four of his most remarkable and original works, although Dylan referred to them later as 'his apples carved in oil, his sulphurously glowing lemons, his infernal kippers'. He was rewarded with a hanging of three paintings at the prestigious Mayor Gallery in Mayfair in 1937, alongside, among others, Miró, Braque, Picasso, Klee, Dufy, Bonnard, Matisse and, from England, Paul Nash and Walter Sickert. The exhibition was reviewed in *The Times*, singling Fred out for praise.

> Mr Alfred Janes is a new name to us, and his three paintings reveal both a highly original taste in colour, and an interesting cultivation of textures, an incised line being used to define the forms. 'Soles', light and dark, laid head to tail, is a simple but remarkably effective composition. Mr Janes is a welcome discovery.

But Fred was ready to move on from this method of painting. 'This became complicated – too complicated and restricting,' he concluded. 'I couldn't paint anything that wasn't hexagonal.' And it was slow work. The final work that he made in this way, *Salome*, took him the whole of 1938. It was a hopeless way to try and earn a living. But unlike Dylan, Fred had a part-time teaching job at the art school to keep his head above water. 'Tell Fred he's right,' Dylan wrote to their old school friend Charlie Fisher on Fred's decision to return to Wales. In spring 1938 he used $40 New Directions sent him to rent Eros, an appropriately named but damp and dingy little cottage in Laugharne. At least it looked out at the back across the Taf estuary, and Caitlin could indulge in her passion for swimming. Dylan quickly fell into a routine of visiting Brown's Hotel in the morning for a beer – usually on tick, like nearly all their household expenditure – but mainly to revel in the latest gossip about the goings-on in the village from Ivy Williams, the landlady. After lunch at home he would work all afternoon and then go back to the pub in the evening with Caitlin. They were soon able to move to a nicer house, Sea View. It was a very different pattern to the unsettled, itinerant life that Dylan had been leading for the last five years, as Charlie Fisher noted in his diary after a visit in 1938. 'Drove Dylan and Caitlin to Laugharne, stayed the night, very dull. Was shown a collection of shells.' Caitlin was discovering – as many of his old school friends knew – that beneath the raffish exterior, Dylan was a fairly conventional man. In the evenings he liked to have his slippers laid out by the fire in the sitting room, where he would sit in an armchair and read the paper or the detective novels that he devoured, with a selection of savoury titbits to nibble, provided by Caitlin.

The peace and quiet of Laugharne enabled him to produce a different, more accessible kind of writing that appealed to a much wider audience. *The Map of Love*, a collection of stories and poems published in 1939, reflected a preoccupation with relationships: 'I make this in a warring absence' is about the jealous feelings his love for Caitlin could arouse, and 'After the funeral' a tribute to his Aunt Ann, who had died of cancer, 'Her fist of a face died clenched on a round pain'. Short stories like 'A Visit to Grandpa's' and 'The Peaches', evoking the boyhood pleasures of his Carmarthenshire holidays, would provide the contents of one of his most enjoyable volumes, *Portrait of the Artist as a Young Dog* (a play on the title of James Joyce's novel), published in 1940. His first book in the US was handsomely produced and published in 1939, a collection of short stories and poems entitled *The World I Breathe*, and favourably reviewed by important American poets like Robert Lowell and John Berryman.

Vernon visited Eros to work on poems together – sometimes at the urgent request of Dylan – travelling the forty miles from Swansea by bus or bicycle. He often brought gifts of food, books or money and even a radio so that his host could listen to the cricket scores. Vernon later said that he thought that this was the happiest time of Dylan's life and wrote a poem about him, 'Portrait of a Friend'. Caitlin agreed, despite their newly-married tiffs. She was now expected to behave like the dutiful, if impecunious, wife, making broth with free bones from the butcher that she would keep on the stove in a huge black iron pot and top up with carrots, potatoes, turnips and leeks. 'It would simmer gently from one week's end to the next, often turning a rather nasty shade of blue.' Her support enabled Dylan to write, but it scuppered her dreams of becoming a professional dancer in the mode of Isadora Duncan, whose revolutionary, free-spirited, flowing style of movement she had studied. The frustration and disappointment sometimes bubbled over, as Vernon observed. On one occasion she threw his gift of a bag of plums one by one at Dylan when he refused to clear the table after their meal because he and Vernon had more important work to do.

Caitlin would soon have more responsibilities: much to their surprise, she was pregnant, the baby due early the next year. But something far more momentous was on the horizon. 'The hand that signed the paper' was prophetic: in September 1938 the Treaty of Munich, signed by Britain, France, Italy and Germany, allowed Hitler to annex part of Czechoslovakia. Everyone knew that war was inevitable. Dylan's poem at the end of that year, 'A saint about

81

to fall', expressed his anxiety at bringing a child into a world on the brink of destruction. The last painting that Fred completed before war broke out, *The Queue*, reflected the prevailing sense of dread. Whether Dylan and his school friends had decided to live in London or Wales was irrelevant. Swansea's Bohemians would be scattered far and wide and the notes arranging to meet on Fred's studio wall would soon go up in smoke.

PART TWO

THE POINT OF NO RETURN

Dylan Thomas by Alfred Janes, 1953.
The poet died before the portrait was completed

CHAPTER SIX

THE PARTY'S OVER

The old coach house has been converted into a rudimentary studio, its rough stone floor covered over with planks to make a walkway. Holes in the roof deliver pinpricks of light boosted by bare electric bulbs strung on wires between the wooden beams, and more light seeps in through the gap between the top of the walls and the roof. A paraffin heater struggles against the early winter chill, but Fred is still wearing his vest and pyjamas under a thick Welsh tweed suit topped with his old army gaiters and a thick brown leather jerkin in an effort to keep warm. He is painting Dylan for a second time, but his old friend is not sitting for the portrait. Fred has had to finish it from memory and photographs, because Dylan Thomas is dead.

The slightly hollow cheeks of the 1934 portrait have filled out and the youthful halo of curls is cropped and darker. But the brown eyes still gaze out intently, and while Dylan's frame has expanded, thanks to beer and sweets, his fingers are still slim and elegant. 'His small, narrow, hands were white and long-fingered, as artists' hands are supposed to be,' as Caitlin said. Why Fred, who was now living with his wife Mary and young son Ross in an old farmhouse on the Gower peninsula, had decided to paint Dylan again at this time is not clear. The portrait does not acknowledge what bad shape Dylan was in before falling into a coma and dying aged thirty-nine, allegedly of alcohol poisoning, in a hospital in New York on 9 November 1953. Perhaps Fred wanted to preserve a different kind of image. 'I've known every detail of his face since he sat for the portrait I did while I was a student at the Royal Academy Schools,' he said to Mary. In less than fifteen years, the increasingly successful young poet living in a sleepy Welsh village, with a woman he loved passionately and a baby on the way, had become a physical wreck locked in a mutually destructive marriage. How did the best become the worst of times?

You couldn't blame the war. Of course Dylan and his grammar school friends suffered the consequences of so much death and destruction, but they all survived, and in some ways it was the making of Dylan. The universal themes of birth and death, love and loss that infused his inner spiritual world were now a horrifyingly real part of everyday life. Little music, poetry or art was produced by his close contemporaries, who all served in the armed forces, but Dylan wrote some of his most moving poetry during the conflict, and contributed in his own way to the war effort by working on radio broadcasts for the BBC and films for companies contracted to the Ministry of Information – more than 200 moral-raising productions in all.

As war became inevitable Dylan tried to offer his services as a writer to various official bodies. Active service was not something he could contemplate. 'To him no one country was better than another, all men were equal regardless of race or religion, and he recognised no boundaries between people,' Caitlin explained. 'The whole notion of war was ridiculous to him and he told me that he would never, ever under any circumstances, kill a human being...' But joining the ranks of the conscientious objectors, whom he believed, refused to fight for all the wrong reasons, was not acceptable either: he wasn't prepared to do nothing. At the suggestion of Augustus John, he wrote pleading letters to Sir Kenneth Clark, the art historian and writer (and father of the future Conservative minister Alan Clark), who was director of the film division at the Ministry of Information, to ask for some sort of 'exempting work'. An attempt to join a planned private anti-aircraft battery set up by a friend of Clark's stalled.

It was a desperate situation. Dylan now had his baby son Llewelyn, born in January 1939, as well as Caitlin to support with very little income. 'Its name is Llewelyn Thomas,' he wrote to Vernon Watkins a couple of days after the birth. 'It is red-faced, very angry & blue-eyed. Bit blue, bit green. It does not like the world.' The publication of *The Map of Love*, only days before war was declared on 3 September, had gone almost unnoticed. Dylan's dream of becoming a successful freelance poet and writer was now looking hopeless. According to Caitlin, he found a way out by contriving to fail his army medical at the end of April 1940 by getting rip-roaring drunk the night before at Brown's Hotel. 'The next morning he came out in spots and was shaking and coughing his guts up,' she claimed. 'At one stage, he even fainted. They classified him C3, right down to the bottom of the list.' He would only be called up as a very last resort.

It solved one problem, but not how they were going to survive. The first German bombs aimed at Swansea's vital port and refineries forty miles away were lighting up the skies near Laugharne, so a safe haven at his parents' house was not an option. Caitlin's family came to the rescue yet again. The new parents had gone to stay in Hampshire for help with the arrival of Llewelyn, and now scuttled back to the Macnamara household to avoid creditors in Laugharne. Their goodwill and even the vegetable broth had finally run out. To pay off his debts, Dylan had to resort to persuading influential friends like the sculptor Henry Moore and the poets Stephen Spender and Henry Reed to write to some wealthy subscribers of the leading magazine *Horizon* asking for a suggested £70 donation to help him. They raised £126 12s 0d (about two thirds of the average annual salary at the time). The young family would not live in Laugharne again until after the war, which saw them moving around continually between London, Swansea, Hampshire and anywhere else that could provide a roof over their heads.

By now Dylan's poems were being read on the radio, and he had taken part in a couple of BBC broadcasts, although it took eighteen months to be invited back after the first one, 'Life and the Modern Poet', as he was in a pub in London when he was supposed to be in a Swansea studio recording it. Luckily a friend tracked him down and a link was hastily established from the capital to Wales. His fellow guests in the second broadcast, 'The Modern Muse', were Louis MacNeice, W.H. Auden, Kathleen Raine and Stephen Spender – all notable poets of the day and at least five years senior to 23-year-old Dylan. It showed how swiftly his star was rising.

The government banned the launch of new magazines in 1940 to conserve precious paper supplies, but it needed scriptwriters for documentaries that the Ministry of Information was churning out to raise morale. Dylan contacted one of the London production companies it commissioned, but the start of the Blitz on the capital scuppered his efforts. The bombing terrified and repelled Dylan. A frightening night when he got caught up in a raid inspired a poem called 'Deaths and Entrances', which he worked on that autumn with Vernon, who was still in Pennard. The bank was unwilling to release its cashier so he had not yet been called up. The poem was published in *Horizon* in January 1941, but according to Vernon's wife Gwen, Dylan regretted a suggestion of Vernon's to use the word 'zodiac', 'because Zodiac is a Watkins word, not a Thomas word,' Dylan grumbled. 'Deaths and Entrances' later became the title poem of probably his most popular collection, published soon after the war ended.

The young family had been leading their usual peripatetic lifestyle, staying briefly with Dylan's parents in Bishopston on the

Gower peninsula and then in the summer of 1940 at The Maltings, an artists' and writers' colony in Gloucestershire countryside, set up by Dylan's friend the poet John Davenport. Here they worked on a spoof satirical thriller called *The Death of the King's Canary*, about the death of the Poet Laureate. Dylan loved thrillers and he was delighted by the idea of sending up every cliché in the genre. He had started working on it originally with his former grammar school friend and newspaper colleague Charlie Fisher, who had now enlisted, and, appropriately, written in verse to let Dylan know that he was joining the Army Intelligence Corps.

The poet Charlie Fisher
Will be compelled to join the militia
With a lot of other pricks
On June sixth

Dylan and Davenport continued the pastiches of famous poets and lampoons of important cultural figures – Cyril Connolly, editor of *Horizon*, was disguised as Basil Minto, while Augustus John became Hercules Jones. Caitlin, meanwhile, found herself spending long periods of time alone, Llewelyn having been left with her mother at Blashford, an expedience that turned into an almost permanent arrangement over the years to come. Her only means of expression was practising her dancing in the chapel at The Maltings, but without the audience she craved. There was a more pressing need: despite her passionate relationship with Dylan, she claimed never to have reached orgasm with him. And she suspected – rightly – that he did not always spend the night alone on his London work trips. Two could play at that game.

One of the other guests at The Maltings was a charismatic pianist and critic called William Glock (who later became a ground-breaking controller of music at the BBC). She enjoyed listening to the handsome, blond musician play Schubert and Mozart beautifully and they formed a romantic liaison, which Caitlin described in carefully chosen words. 'There was a feeling between us … like falling in love and we conceived this idea of having one night of love in Cardiff: it was the first time I had ever calculated an infidelity.' Her pretext was a long-overdue visit to see her in-laws, D.J. and Florence, in Swansea, which Dylan fell for. But with no money to buy alluring clothes for her night of passion, she fitted in a trip to Laugharne to sell all their Welsh blankets and crockery and spent the money on a 'super outfit' in Cardiff. Her expectations ended in humiliation. After drinks and dinner Caitlin got into bed beside Glock in her Isadora tunic – only to remain flat on her back in total silence, Glock alongside her, motionless, until she fell asleep. Not a word was said in the morning.

Florence was not stupid and while she normally turned a blind eye to Dylan's unconventional behaviour, she realised that a night in Caitlin's trip was unaccounted for and wrote to him. When he realised what had gone on, Caitlin's revenge did not taste so sweet: he threw a knife at her, refused to speak and took her and Llewelyn straight to Blashford. His growing anxiety about marriage and the strain of living through a war is reflected in 'On a wedding anniversary', published at the start of the following year:

The sky is torn across
This ragged anniversary of two
Who moved for three years in tune
Down the long walks of their vows.

Now their love lies a loss
And Love and his patients roar on a chain;
From every true or crater
Carrying cloud, Death strikes their house.

Too late in the wrong rain
They come together whom their love parted:
The windows pour into their heart
And the doors burn in their brain.

Dylan's prospects of paid work were not faring any better. He was working on a collection of stories, but told Vernon he was unhappy about dashing it off. *Adventures in the Skin Trade* was later rejected by Dent because it was not well written enough. A £50 grant from the Literary Fund in early 1941 disappeared all too quickly, and the family was forced to go and stay with D.J. and Florence over the winter – not as very welcome guests because they mislaid their ration books. Vernon, who had been rejected by the Field Security Police because the motorbike he was expected to ride during the interview just kept going around in circles, was very pleased to see Dylan again and even lent him his precious typewriter so that he could keep working.

*'Our Swansea has died,' Dylan said of the devastation of
his hometown in a three night Blitz in February 1941*

The old Swansea they all knew would soon disappear forever. In February 1941 a three-night blitz dropped more than 1,000 explosives and 56,000 incendiary bombs on the town. They missed the docks and refineries, but killed 230 people and destroyed the Kardomah Cafe and many of Dylan's favourite drinking haunts along with most of the town centre. Vernon was in the Home Guard, and watched the blaze from his post on top of a Gower hillside. Charlie Fisher was stationed on the Somerset coast and saw a great plume of smoke across the water. When he asked what it was he was told it was Swansea burning. Bert Trick, Dylan's left-wing grocer friend, was now an air raid warden and worked in the office that helped people acquire bomb shelters. 'I stood on the corner facing where the office had been the night before, and there was nothing but a heaving mass of smouldering buildings.' As he stood there, Dylan and Caitlin came around the corner. 'Bert, our Swansea had died,' he said. 'Our Swansea has died.'

Self-portrait in uniform by Alfred Janes, 1942, one of the few works that Janes was able to produce during the Second World War

CHAPTER SEVEN

FRIENDS AND ENEMIES

Few of Dylan's closest friends witnessed the destruction of their hometown. Fred, like Dylan, could not contemplate killing another human being, but abhorred Hitler and his fascist regime. He avoided jail by joining the non-combatant lowly Pioneer Corps on the grounds that his short-sightedness classified him as having 'defective vision', much to the amusement of those who recognised his prize-winning skills as an artist. The corps were the army's labourers and workmen who prepared the way for active troops, mopped up behind them and dealt with the aftermath of bombing raids. Many of them were ex-convicts, poorly educated, or refugees from Europe who spoke little English. Fred decided that if he was going to have to dig latrines, they would be very good latrines. He soon starting winning his stripes, and was commissioned before long.

Dylan had written to Vernon from Gloucestershire for news of the wartime diaspora. 'What are our old Swansea friends doing? Is Fred still crossgartering fruit and faces? drilling? objecting? I don't hear from him ever. Life & Letter of course.' Fred rarely wrote letters and Dylan was referring to a joke a friend had made about publishing a book called the *Life & Letter of Alfred Janes*. In fact Fred spent the first few weeks of his service in Oldham in the north of England, training in some cotton mills where 'all we seemed to do was march all day'. Dylan asked Vernon for his address, poking fun affectionately at Fred's meticulous working methods. 'I'd like to write to him, even tho he won't answer. I'll enjoy seeing his war pictures: the veins of a leaf that blew from a shelled tree; the crisscrosses on the head of a spent bullet. He should do widespread camouflage work & make Oldham look like the back of a herring.'

Fred and his company travelled all over the country, digging trenches, erecting barbed wire, repairing dry stone walls that had been knocked down on tank exercises, and after a course on demolition, clearing up after bombing raids. In Liverpool, the smoke created by incendiary bombs enveloped the city in a darkness to last for days. Dylan may have enjoyed his running joke about his friend's aversion to letter writing, but Fred sent hundreds to Mary over the course of the war, often writing every few days. They were full of boredom, frustration at army bureaucracy, worries about getting paid and longing for the next bit of leave and his new wife, whom he clearly adored. Memories of happy times and imagining the future with a beloved partner kept many soldiers sane during wartime separation, Fred among them.

'God how I would have chafed under these circumstances ten years ago when I was always half mad with impatience to "live" and "do"; now I feel more resigned and I have you to think about,' he wrote from Northumberland in 1941. 'I think that to live here without having someone who mattered greatly deep down inside you would be torture, absolute torture.' For Fred, just the act of writing letters had a special role. 'The sheer making of a letter supplies something that is so very necessary to me, who is so used to making things.'

The government wanted to record the everyday lives of citizens during the war, and the War Artists Advisory Committee, the body responsible for commissioning art, looked favourably on photographs that Fred arranged to send them of his work. The committee wrote to his commanding officer asking that he be 'afforded such facilities for sketching as are consistent with the performance of his military duties,' and wanted more examples of his work 'with a view to purchase and in any case subject to censorship'. The request was passed on, with a cheeky enquiry as to whether he could 'render a specimen for a group Christmas card' as soon as possible. Fred's hope was to keep painting by returning to Swansea and recording the destruction of the town, but nothing came of it. At one stage he was stationed on the Redesdale estate in Northumberland, where he drew a pencil portrait of the eccentric 2nd Baron, David Freeman-Mitford, a fascist sympathiser until the outbreak of war and father of the Mitford sisters, Diana, Jessica, Unity, Nancy, Deborah and Pamela. It was one of only a handful of pictures that Fred would produce over the whole six-year length of his army service. Another was a pencil self-portrait in uniform, a third of Mary.

Mary Janes, the artist's wife, by Alfred Janes, 1942

They had married in Swansea's Guildhall on 9 November 1940, when Fred was able to snatch a few days' special leave at very short notice. Mary's sister, Ethel Ross, described their wedding in a short memoir entitled *Venus and Mars*. The bride had little time to buy an outfit, but found a grey suit with a pale pink stripe that fitted her lovely figure perfectly and a soft cashmere blouse to go underneath. No hat, however, as her boss had not allowed her to leave early enough to get to the milliner's before it shut for the blackout. 'Mother, Mary and I,' Ethel wrote, 'watched Fred clatter up the ceremonial steps, striking sparks with his hobnailed army boots, looking seven feet tall in his great coat. Sparks at both ends now, I thought, recalling his formidable prowess in debate with the wits and the wags who met in the Kardomah for coffee in the mornings.' None of them was able to come at such short notice, and some had already enlisted or been called up. 'So Fred and Mary had none of the usual wedding jokers to jolly them with horseshoes and slippers. Everyone there was solemn and fearful.'

The little party, which included Fred's mother and a few new friends who found themselves living in Swansea during the war, enjoyed a wedding breakfast of a large tin of assorted cheese biscuits, which were still unrationed, and sherry, 'a cardinal sin to the older generation of Janeses, all chapel goers'. A tin of ham sent from Canada by Donald, one of Ethel and Mary's four brothers who had all left the country during the slump to find work, was very welcome. The couple drove off for a very brief honeymoon in a little Ford car that Fred's mother had bought him. That was probably the last Fred saw of the Swansea he knew. The blitz destroyed his studio, and along with it all his special paint recipes, which he had written on the walls instead of bits of paper, for safekeeping. His mother-in-law had also gone missing. Mrs Ross was in Swansea hospital having a routine operation when the bombs fell. Many years later, Mary recalled how she made her way through the smoking ruins of the town, defying the wardens to try and find out if her mother had survived. It was some time before the two sisters heard that she had been evacuated along with other patients up into the valleys for safety, but died in the ambulance.

The absent wedding guests were by now all doing their bit for Britain. Vernon Watkins had finally joined the RAF police in 1941, where he managed to go eighteen months without ever making an arrest. Whenever the opportunity arose to book someone for coming back to camp drunk or late, he would have his head stuck in a book. He passed the time on night patrols at his camp in Uxbridge by writing poems in his head, but always kept to the camp perimeter because he got hopelessly lost inside. 'Vernon, who knew every rock and gully in Gower, seemed to be completely at sea anywhere else,' his wife Gwen wrote in her wartime memoir *Cracking the Luftwaffe Codes*.

A clever but determined young woman who loved English and was destined for university, Gwen Davies applied instead to join the Women's Auxiliary Air Force (WAAF) on her seventeenth birthday, but was not called up until 1942. After a few months training and clerical work, twenty-year-old Gwen was mysteriously dumped by a military driver in front of some imposing gates with no idea where she was, or why. A guard explained that this was Bletchley Park. 'And if you want to know what that is,' added his colleague, 'it's the biggest lunatic asylum in Britain'. Its residents may not have been mad, but Bletchley Park, home of the Second World War codebreakers was, Gwen soon realised, inhabited by 'glorious eccentrics, brilliant wits, men and women of outstanding intellect, even genius'. Two of them were Dan Jones and Vernon Watkins.

Vernon had also arrived in 1942. He was just as inept, Gwen

observed, marching into a broom cupboard time and again after 'pay parade' when servicemen picked up their wages. He failed to win a commission because, while he did extremely well in the written tests, during the drill he marched his squad into a brick wall when he forgot to say 'About turn!', and omitted to take his rifle with him on parade. 'I didn't really want to be an officer anyway,' he told Gwen. 'You get much better table tennis in the sergeants' mess.' Vernon's lack of military prowess was compensated for by the appearance of his first volume of poetry, *The Ballad of the Mari Lwyd*, the previous year. The title poem is based on an old Welsh tradition of travelling from house to house with someone dressed as a horse, singing songs and wishing the occupiers good luck in the hope of being rewarded with food and drink. Apart from the cachet of being published by T.S. Eliot at Faber & Faber, the collection was reviewed very favourably in the *Times Literary Supplement* and *The Spectator*. A future Swansea-born Archbishop of Canterbury, Rowan Williams, would describe the ballad as 'one of the outstanding poems of the century'.

There was something else to be thankful for. One day in the canteen at Bletchley, Vernon noticed a young man with a mop of curly hair and round glasses. 'You are Dan Jones, aren't you?' he asked. Dylan had described his close friend the composer so clearly that Vernon's guess was right. He was delighted to meet at last someone whom Dylan had talked about so much. Vernon and Dan soon became friends too, but could only meet in the canteen or on days off. Dan was already a captain, and ran a section translating and decoding Japanese. He was also working on a Japanese–Chinese dictionary. 'His brain', as Gwen said, 'was astounding'. He and Vernon enjoyed playing word games together and Vernon was fascinated by Dan's descriptions of Chinese ideograms.

Dan was lucky enough to have a billet on a farm, where he enjoyed hearty produce at mealtimes and cakes baked for him by the farmer's daughters. Gwen and Vernon were invited for supper there once. 'We had homemade sausages of inconceivable deliciousness, jacket potatoes with butter and fresh broad beans, with a currant tart to follow' – a feast for appetites that were rarely satisfied by army rations. With an eye on developing survival skills in case of an invasion, Dan also invented his own dishes, sometimes based on squirrel or snails, that he cooked in an iron pot over the fireplace in his cosy quarters.

Vernon and Dylan kept writing to each other during the early stages of the war, although Dylan, hurtfully, failed to acknowledge a copy of *The Ballad of the Mari Lwyd* that Vernon sent him, or its favourable reviews. Many of Dylan's letters to Vernon asked for loans, or expressed gratitude for his unfailing generosity. Llewelyn was Vernon's godson, and he had written some poems dedicated to the boy that were published in *Life and Letters* magazine. With typical generosity, he gave the fee to Dylan for the overdue hire purchase payments on the double bed he shared with Caitlin. Dylan joked that Llewelyn would own half a leg. It was easy to lose touch with friends during wartime, especially for Dylan and Caitlin, who moved around so much. In summer 1941 they were back in Laugharne, staying with their writer friend Richard Hughes at Castle House. Here, Dylan was delighted to come across an old letter from Charlie Fisher, whose address Dylan had lost. He wrote immediately. 'I thought I'd better write at once, before I found a drawing of Fred's (Still Life: one Egg June 1936–June 1940) behind the hat rack in the music room, or a manuscript of Tom's (Mabinogion, a Tone Poem for Horn and Kardomah) behind the butler in the cook's room.'

Much to Dylan's relief, Strand Films finally offered him a job in the autumn to work on their government propaganda films, which were shown along with newsreels in the cinema – hardly anyone owned a TV, which had been shut down in any case at the start of the war. There were concerns that transmissions across the airwaves would help enemy bombers identify central London, and in any case, technical staff would be needed in wartime operations. The worst of the bombing had subsided, and Dylan felt brave enough to return to London and take up Strand's offer of contributing ideas, scripts and voiceovers, for which he would receive £10 a week – an above-average income for the time. Spending more time in London meant he could meet Swansea friends on leave like Fred, or John Prichard, who was in the Navy, for drinks in the Fitzroy Tavern. Vernon and Dan could travel from Bletchley to London on days off. Dylan had lost touch with Dan when the young composer was on his Mendelssohn travelling scholarship, and they had had little chance to meet during the war until now. Before being transferred to the Intelligence Corps, Dan was in the Royal Corps of Signals – the army's communicators – and prior to Bletchley he had been posted all over the country. His reunions in London with Dylan were not a happy revival of the Warmley days, however.

'I would have been wise not to seek Dylan out at all during those short leaves from Bletchley,' Dan wrote in his memoir, *My Friend Dylan Thomas*. 'It was impossible to detach him from a new circle of acquaintances, some of whom treated me with less than courtesy.' He partly blamed his smart captain's uniform (he had no civilian clothes), which made him stand out, but also his admitted 'tendency to deliver lectures on almost all subjects,' some of them very unfashionable. 'This is the chap who actually *likes* Wagner,' was how one of Dylan's circle described him. 'I also like Couperin, Mussorgsky, Fauré, Johann Strauss Junior, and I have a surname as well as a Christian name,' Dan replied testily. Dylan was now, as Dan recognised, 'a famous man and often in the centre of an admiring circle,' and 'shuffling round on the periphery' of it left Dan, understandably, feeling a tad left out. It would be several years before they became close friends again.

Tom Warner by Alfred Janes, 1946. A musician,
he was a close schoolfriend of the artist and Thomas

CHAPTER EIGHT

WE'LL MEET AGAIN

Wartime London appealed to Dylan. Apart from the chance, finally, of earning a regular income, its heady, 'anything goes' atmosphere was highly attractive. Members of the establishment, soldiers on leave and European refugees rubbed shoulders with low-life types and arty Bohemians in Soho's bars and clubs. It was the kind of shifting social mix that Dylan loved, and his personal qualities could instantly put whatever company he chose at ease, as Fred recognised.

> His empathy with the world and those around him was complete and he responded to his surroundings in such a way as sometimes to give the impression that he comprised multiple, diverse personalities – each one a stranger to the rest. He could be punctilious, outrageous, comic, tragic, or just totally unexceptional. The intelligentsia, the bartenders and even the herons could easily take him as one of themselves.

Dylan's output was prodigious at Strand Films, where he wrote at least a dozen scripts. Many were straightforward morale-raising efforts, including one which he also produced, called *Wales – Green Mountain, Black Mountain*, that showed how different workers, from sheep farmers to miners, were contributing to the war effort. Another, *Balloon Site 568*, intended to recruit women to train as operators of the barrage balloons that deterred enemy aircraft, offered less promising material, and now seems like a modern TV

105

comedy sketch sending up the genre. Sometimes his ideas were too near the knuckle for the censors, however, including one that poked fun at the government slogan 'Is your journey really necessary?'. Titled 'Is your Ernie really necessary', and involving a dancing chorus line, it was banned by the censor. Some of Dylan's output was harder hitting, including *These Are the Men*, in which Nazi leaders rant about their fascist leanings over footage of their 1934 Nuremberg rally, infamously filmed by Leni Riefenstahl. *The Spectator* described it as 'the most pitiless condemnation of individual Nazi leaders that has yet appeared in the cinema'. It certainly conveys Dylan's utter contempt for the regime and his ability to ridicule authoritarian figures.

Living in London also made it easier for Dylan to get work at the BBC, where there was increased demand for writers and presenters. In the 1930s, broadcasts had not started until the evening – now they were on all day. They were not always very entertaining, as Gwen Watkins pointed out. 'All the talks were usually about how to make compost out of seaweed, or whether Bach the younger was as good as so and so.' Dylan's poems and talks were a breath of fresh air for listeners needing distraction from the hardship of wartime life. His funny and affectionate memoir 'Reminiscences of Childhood', read with warmth and none of the booming oratory style that he is usually remembered for, included a reading of 'The hunchback in the park', and introduced listeners to the Swansea of his youth and his much-quoted description of it as an 'ugly, lovely town'.

Never *was* there such a town (I thought) for the smell of fish and chips on Saturday nights, for the Saturday afternoon cinema matinees, where we shouted and hissed our threepences away; for the crowds in the streets, with leeks in their pockets, on international [rugby] nights ... for the park, the inexhaustibly ridiculous and mysterious, the bushy, Red-Indian hiding park...

Dylan was also sought after as a public speaker and was invited to address the English Club at Oxford University, where the young Philip Larkin described being in the audience. 'Hell of a fine man: little, snubby, hopelessly pissed bloke who made hundreds of cracks and read parodies of everybody in appropriate voices.' Dylan was reading from *The Death of the King's Canary*, the spoof thriller he had been working on with John Davenport. He may have had some members of the audience rolling on the floor with laughter, but others were offended by the grosser elements of his talk and tried to drag him out of the party afterwards and throw him in a pond.

His career as a writer and performer was on a firmer footing, but at home things were shakier. Dylan may have been earning £10 a week, but it disappeared very quickly, partly because of his Robin Hood-like attitude to money and possessions. 'He didn't mind robbing the rich – he would steal their shirts or their money quite happily,' Gwen explained. 'When he had money he was tremendously generous.' Vernon recalled a Christmas in London when Dylan had just received a cheque that he cashed and spent on presents of books, toys, champagne and chocolates, when he owed money to the butcher and baker. 'He was child-like in that respect,' Gwen believed. 'He wanted happiness and he wanted it now.' He was also happy to indulge Caitlin's love of fancy clothes – of a £40 cheque he received when they were deep in debt, she spent fourteen guineas on a gold swimming costume, in which, Gwen admitted, she looked stunning. Some of his generosity was undoubtedly dispensed in the pub. He was now spending more time drinking with his BBC pals, pitching for work from producers who were mostly Oxford-educated public schoolboys, and among whom he probably felt rather insecure. 'I thought it was very tiring to sell yourself to editors and BBC people,' said Gwen, who observed some of these encounters at first hand. 'Sometimes I thought that was why he drank so much.'

Caitlin was well aware that the professional opportunities that wartime London offered her husband might also lead him astray. With nowhere to live, the offer of a warm bed for the night was often an attractive option – sometimes the only option. Caitlin recognised that while Dylan was a flirt, he was not really a womaniser – but he was very easy to seduce. So she decided to join him in London and leave Llewelyn with her mother and her sister Brigit at Blashford. 'Leaving Llewelyn was quite traumatic, quite the most painful thing that ever happened to me,' she wrote, 'because I had been so in love with this baby and so possessive … but I felt that if I didn't, Dylan would drift back into that pub life that he had before he met me'. Things did not quite turn out as she envisaged, however. Caitlin was the trained performer, but Dylan got all the attention. His drunken pub antics sickened her, but according to Gwen, she would flirt with men in uniform to get her own back. The result would often be Dylan attacking someone much bigger, and usually coming off worst. At one party, Caitlin, all too familiar with the effects of his charm on women, stubbed out a cigarette on the hand of one of her (wrongly) presumed rivals.

The couple found a base in a dilapidated one-room studio in Manresa Road in Chelsea vacated by Dan, who lent them his books and furniture. Although the rent was only £1 a week, Dylan's earnings quickly disappeared. Air raids still terrified him and once when Vernon came to stay, a particularly heavy bombardment began. They crouched under the table, Dylan shivering in fear, while Vernon, a devout Christian, tried to calm him by talking about the immortality of the soul. On another occasion they were in a taxi that narrowly missed being hit by a V-1 flying bomb. Dylan was less afraid of dying than being found dead with a copy of the popular newspaper *Reveille* open on the pages carrying 'pin-ups' of scantily clad women. The philosophical Vernon had no such qualms as 'I always have Kierkegaard in my pocket'.

When Dylan and Caitlin needed to get out of London, his old Swansea friends the Phillips family were among the many people who put them up. Vera had come to London to study design and supported herself with acting and waitressing jobs, but her family had left Swansea for rural Carmarthenshire to escape the bombs. Their country home was a welcome retreat for Caitlin, who was pregnant again and longed for fresh air, peace and quiet. The house was not far from the little seaside town of New Quay in Cardiganshire – where both Vera and Caitlin would make more permanent homes. Her baby girl was born in London in March 1943 and named Aeronwy, or Aeron for short, after a river which flows through the countryside near the Phillipses' house. Dylan was nowhere to be seen. Few fathers were present at the birth of their children in those days – even fewer during wartime – but they didn't all wait a week until coming to see their baby, and then turn up at the hospital in an old dressing gown and slippers, looking 'shagged out', as Caitlin claimed. Neither was he at Manresa Road to greet them when they got home. Caitlin was horrified to find the place littered with dirty dishes, beer bottles and fag ends. 'I only had to take one look at our crumpled bed to realise that Dylan had had some other woman in it while I'd been in hospital.'

As her family responsibilities grew, Dylan's absences, philandering and feckless attitude to money became more painful, frustrating and, inevitably, more damaging. The only thing that stopped her leaving, she said, was her wonder at how beautiful her baby was: 'perfectly angelic, with such beautiful curly hair even then'. But Caitlin was also guilty of neglect. Llewelyn was arguably safer in Hampshire, but Aeron was often left alone in the studio, which had a glass roof, while Caitlin and Dylan went out drinking. While the life of wartime mothers was unimaginably hard compared to today – Caitlin, for example, washed all Aeronwy's nappies by hand and hung them out to dry in a bombed-out building opposite – it is difficult to empathise with her reasoning: 'Had I not gone to the pub with Dylan I would have been left there, sitting like a fool.' In 1944 she decamped to New Quay with Aeron, where Dylan rented a holiday shack on the cliffs above the picturesque little town, while Vera Phillips moved into her family's property next door. Their new home, Dylan wrote to Vernon, was called "Majoda" – made up of the beginnings of the names of the three children of the man who built it. 'I may alter the name to "Catllewdylaer"', he quipped.

Dylan was trying to finish a film script that he had been commissioned to write, *The Doctor and the Devils*, based on the life of the Victorian grave robbers Burke and Hare, which gave him the excuse to disappear up to London. But back in Wales, near the sea, in a more domesticated and less distracting set-up, his poetry and prose began to change. In 1941 he had sold his precious notebooks to the State University of New York in Buffalo via a Swansea book dealer, who was paid £35 for them before commission. The money was one reason for the sale, but Dylan had also told Caitlin that he was relying on the notebooks too much as source material and needed to write fresh, new work. What Caitlin described as 'one of the most creative periods of his life' began. He was, as she pointed out, 'always at his best when alone with his own resources'.

He produced a handful of sobering, deeply moving war poems reflecting his experiences, including 'A Refusal to Mourn the Death, by Fire, of a Child in London'. 'In my craft or sullen art' was a kind of personal miniature manifesto, which stated his aim of writing poetry 'Not for ambition or bread / Or the strut and trade of charms / On the ivory stages…', but only for lovers 'Who pay no praise or wages / nor heed my craft or art'. Another poem from this time is 'This side of the truth', written for Llewelyn. 'King of your blue eyes / In the blinding country of youth' reveals a man thinking deeply about the innocence of childhood and what was, to him, its inevitable corruption. A decade later, when Fred was coming to terms with being a father, he painted a picture with the same title, adding '(Parenthood)' to it.

Dylan had also been visiting the Llansteffan peninsula again, where Florence and D.J. had moved to a family cottage, Blaencwm. Here he wrote 'Fern Hill' and 'Poem in October' – marking his thirtieth birthday in 1944. He had always made rough workings and jottings on sheet after sheet of paper and while there are 250 for 'Poem in October' alone, both are less complex than many earlier poems but richly evocative of the natural world of his childhood, as well as melancholic with the awareness of time passing.

> It was my thirtieth year to heaven,
> Woke to my hearing from harbour and neighbour wood
> And the mussel pooled and the heron
> priested shore
> The morning beckon
> With water praying and call of seagull and rook
> And the knock of sailing boats on the net webbed wall
> Myself to set foot
> That second
> In the still sleeping town and set forth.
> (from 'Poem in October')

New Quay not only enabled Dylan to write calmer, more reflective poetry; it provided the characters, barely disguised, for *Quite Early One Morning*, broadcast in 1945. The landlord of the Black Lion pub recalled how a little crowd would gather round Dylan, who would always make notes about the local people he met. 'He never gave an inkling of his connections with all the world-famous people that he knew intimately … he just mixed with us all … it was just a matter of being with us, understanding us.' The landlord also said he never saw him drunk.

111

Quite Early One Morning sees the narrator wandering around a strange seaside town as it wakes up after a stormy night. Comic and poignant by turns, it is the first iteration of an idea that Dylan would rework ten years later into one of his most famous and inventive works, *Under Milk Wood*. Even some of the characters are the same:

> Open the curtains light the fire, what are servants for?
> I am Mrs Ogmore Pritchard and I want another snooze.
> Dust the china, feed the canary, sweep the drawing room floor;
> And before you let the sun in, mind he wipes his shoes.

New Quay had its darker moments, too. "Majoda" was the scene of a bizarre crime when Vera's husband, William Killick, an army officer whom Caitlin christened 'Drunken Waistcoat' because of his penchant for alcohol and fancy clothes, opened fire on Dylan and Caitlin's bungalow and threatened to let off a grenade. Dylan had been best man at the Killicks' wedding, but Bill now (wrongly) suspected Vera, Dylan and Caitlin of a ménage à trois, and was rightly indignant at the amount of money his wife had been spending on their well-oiled lifestyle. Under considerable stress after working behind enemy lines on special operations in Greece, and fuelled by a feisty evening in the pub, Bill confronted the three at Majoda, where Llewelyn and Aeron were asleep in bed, piercing the thin walls with the bullets from his machine gun. No one was hurt; Dylan remained remarkably calm and took the gun from Bill, who said he would let off the grenade if he did not give it back. Dylan did not hesitate in complying.

Calm was restored, but the neighbours had called the police and a trial for attempted murder ensued, with Dylan taking the stand, in which Captain Killick was acquitted. A fictionalised account of the drama appeared later in the 2008 film *The Edge of Love*, produced by Vera's granddaughter, Rebekah Gilbertson. Keira Knightley took the role of Vera and Sienna Miller, one of the UK's most attractive and sought-after actresses, played Caitlin. It was just the kind of affirmation Caitlin craved – but whether she would have approved or not of the portrayal, we will never know.

New Quay lost its charm for Dylan after the episode, and he headed back to London in the summer of 1945, just a year after moving there. Another personal incident also cast a shadow over his professional achievements during this time. In October 1944 Vernon Watkins asked Dylan to be best man at his wedding to Gwen. Despite the wartime separation, the fellow poets met whenever possible to discuss work in progress, or corresponded if they were unable to, and Dylan would ask Vernon for news of Dan Jones at Bletchley, or tell Vernon if he had seen any of the Swansea crowd. Gwen and Vernon read Dylan's poems and stories together in their spare time, and Gwen recalls Vernon handing her 'Poem in October', which Dylan had enclosed in a letter. They were in the mess in Bletchley, with a noisy game of billiards and the radio in the background. 'It was', she said, 'a staggeringly beautiful poem'. The man whose writing she admired so much, however, spoilt her chance of a beautiful wedding day.

The ceremony was to take place in London at St Bartholomew the Great, in the Lady Chapel – the only part where the roof was still intact after bombing raids. The couple had forty-eight hours' leave, but with the hallmark lack of deference to authority of his Swansea peers, Vernon refused to ask his commanding officer for the necessary permission to marry. 'Well sir, I really don't see what business it is of yours when and whom I marry,' he retorted when summoned to explain himself later. A small family gathering assembled before the ceremony for lunch at the Charing Cross Hotel, but where was Dylan? A phone call to the film company where he was now working reassured Vernon that he was on his way to the hotel, but an hour later he had still not arrived. He would be waiting for them at the church, surely. But he wasn't and when the vicar could wait no longer, a last-minute guest stood in. Vernon was desperately hurt. 'That is the end of Dylan as far as I'm concerned,' he told Gwen. She was just starting to understand fully – as Caitlin already did – that despite the very close friendship and literary collaboration, never mind Vernon's willingness to give or lend him money, the relationship meant less to Dylan than it did to Vernon. It was, as Gwen understood, a bitter blow.

It took Dylan four weeks to write and apologise with a list of excuses, including having forgotten to post the letter and finding it in his pocket. Gwen even suspected that he had faked the creases and crumples. When she finally met him in the bar of the Café Royal she did not revise her opinion of him. 'Yes he was witty and his conversation was brilliant, but only at first; as the drink took over the talk seemed amusing only to the equally inebriated audience.' If Caitlin thought that Dylan was at his best when left alone to write, Gwen mirrored her view: London provided work, but it brought out the worst in him.

By the end of the summer of 1945 the war was over. It would be some time before Dylan's old friends were demobbed, but not all returned to Swansea. His oldest friend, Mervyn Levy, had spent the war as an officer in the Royal Army Educational Corps, then worked as an arts lecturer for the War Office with the honorary rank of lieutenant colonel. He worked in Gibraltar and Germany, before returning to the UK to teach. Charlie Fisher, who had been posted to France, got a job as a parliamentary reporter with Reuters in London.

Fred had occasionally met Dylan for a drink in the Fitzroy Tavern when he was on leave, but in summer 1943 the overseas posting that he had dreaded arrived. Mary was by now expecting their first child, a son whom Fred would have to wait two and a half years to meet. Allied victories against Italy and Germany in the north Africa campaign had left thousands of Italian prisoners of war in the desert and Lieutenant Janes was put in charge of some of the camps in which they were held. If he did any drawing or painting in the desert 'where there were even more flies than sand,' it didn't survive, but he had the satisfaction of coming top in Swahili, which he was taught in preparation for leaving, scoring an average of 98.5 per cent in weekly tests. Visits to the museums in Cairo on leave were his only access to art, where the jewellery from Tutankhamun's tomb inspired painting techniques later.

To stave off the boredom, he wrote several times a week to Mary and sent back what treats he could. One parcel arrived packed with butter, olive oil and nylon stockings. She did her best to promote his work, sending photographs to galleries and arranging for pictures to be exhibited. He also struck up a friendship with an interned Italian doctor who was as bored as he was, and to the disapproval of Fred's superiors, they taught each other to speak English and Italian, so that Fred was fluent by the time he left the army. They became lifelong friends, and Fred's linguistic skills would help to promote Dylan and Vernon's work in Italy.

By the spring of 1946, Fred was back in Swansea. Vernon had returned to the bank, while Dan Jones ensconced himself in a cottage in Cornwall for six months and made up for years of enforced silence by writing chamber music 'with furious speed and concentration'. He was now married for a second time, having left his first wife and three daughters for Irene Goodchild, a striking history graduate from Cambridge whom he had met at Bletchley. Unlike Dylan, the promising creative careers of these three men had more or less ground to a halt during the war. It wasn't just their hometown that needed rebuilding.

Dylan Thomas making one of his many BBC broadcasts,
in a studio with the poet Patric Dickinson

CHAPTER NINE

VOICE OF THE BBC

As the war drew to a close, Dylan assembled his *Deaths and Entrances* collection. But Caitlin, now based in Carmarthenshire with Dylan's parents, was desperate for money. Dylan knew that the only hope of earning any regular income meant working for the BBC, as the propaganda film company that had employed him had been wound up. That meant living in London – but where? Caitlin's sister, Nicolette, eventually found them a flat in Markham Square in Chelsea, where she also lived. Her husband, a society painter called Anthony Devas, refused to have them to stay because on previous occasions trusting them with valuable possessions and his drinks cabinet had proved a mistake.

From here Dylan wrote the usual letters seeking work and chasing payments. The BBC agreed to broadcast *Memories of Christmas* in December 1945 – an early version of what became one of Dylan's best-loved works, *A Child's Christmas in Wales* – but only if it was pre-recorded and not broadcast live 'for reasons I do not think I need to enlarge upon,' the head of the children's service stipulated. By Christmas Dylan and Caitlin were broke and turned to a woman whose generosity they would rely on heavily in years to come. Margaret Taylor was the wife of the historian A. J. P. Taylor, whom Dylan had met before the war when Taylor was a lecturer at Manchester University and contributor of left-wing views to the *Manchester Guardian*. Later Taylor became a familiar voice and face on radio and TV history programmes. At first he and Dylan had enjoyed each other's company, but then the academic became sick of Dylan drinking the contents of a beer barrel that he kept in the house, and of Dylan's requests for loans. His wife, on the other hand, an affectionate and maternal woman, had fallen for Dylan's mischievous charm.

They now lived in Oxford, where Taylor was a fellow at Magdalen College, and had a house in the grounds at Holywell Ford. Margaret, who had aspirations as a poet herself, took the homeless Thomas family in, letting them stay in the damp, unheated summer house in the garden beside the river Cherwell, while Aeron slept in the house with the Taylor's children. Llewelyn was still with his grandmother and aunt in Hampshire and when he did come to stay in Oxford his frail, pale state was worrying. He suffered from asthma and seemed anxious, prompting his parents to wonder if a change of climate would suit him. Margaret fussed over the family, cooking all their meals, which Caitlin found unpalatable, welcoming friends like Dan as guests, organising their social life and introducing her protégé to important Oxford contacts, often with embarrassing results. Her husband did not approve. 'I disliked Dylan Thomas intensely,' Taylor wrote in his memoir. 'He was cruel, he was a sponger even when he had money of his own. He went out of his way to hurt those who helped him.' The possessive Caitlin found Margaret irritating, and her husband cold and pompous. 'He seemed to disapprove of everything, including drink, although he had his own special wines set aside for his own cheeses, which we were forbidden to touch.'

But the arrangement suited Dylan. He could escape to London and the BBC by day, for which he made over fifty broadcasts in 1946, earning about £700. He worked with producers like John Arlott, before he became a cricket commentator, and Roy

Campbell and Louis MacNeice, who were also poets. Several of them commented on Dylan's conscientious approach, including Arlott, who said: 'He was never late, he was never drunk and he never did a bad job.' At the end of the working day, if Dylan wasn't going back to Oxford, he would join his colleagues in the pub until they shut at 10 p.m., or later in clubs like the Gargoyle. Charlie Fisher would sometimes go looking for him, egged on by colleagues after they finished work at the House of Commons late in the evening, and find him holding court in exchange for pints from his hangers-on, drunker than all of them. Despite that, he was a formidable presence, puncturing pretentiousness, a cigarette dangling permanently from his lips. But for Charlie, Soho always promised more than it delivered.

Sometimes Dylan would take the train back to Oxford. While Caitlin claimed that Margaret drove him crazy – 'another of those would be female intellectuals' – his gratitude to her was reflected in the trouble he took over their hostess's poetry. A long letter written to her from the guest bedroom at Holywell Ford is totally self-deprecating but revelatory about his own approach to writing poetry. 'I can only burble, like an old bird with its beak full of bias and soap,' he wrote; 'and you can but curse yourself for ever having given your poems to such a turgid rook.' The meaning of a poem, Dylan states, is something that poets can't talk about – that must be left to 'theoreticians, logicians, philosophers, sentimentalists, etc'. Only the texture, made up of sound, shape and colour, could be discussed. Readers do, or don't find poems appeal to them emotionally and the only thing to examine is the words that aroused the emotion. Only the words can be changed until 'the music is made, the music is done, the sound and the spell remain'. His comments are encouraging and reveal how diplomatic Dylan could be when the need arose. 'I like the last verse,' he says of one, 'though there are memories in it, for me, of passages in Eliot: particularly of passages in "Burnt Norton" where he writes of "at the still point of the turning world". The resemblance, mostly of mood, was probably fortuitous and matters very little anyway.'

Although he had little time to write new poetry himself, *Deaths and Entrances* was well received when it was published in February 1946. Edith Sitwell was full of praise in her review in *Our Time* magazine – for which Dylan wrote a grovelling thank-you letter, apologising for having lost touch with her for ten years. It was a sign of his standing that the next time they met was at a poetry reading in May 1946 in front of royalty at the Wigmore Hall in London. Queen Elizabeth and the royal princesses Elizabeth and Margaret listened to work read by leading poets including Sitwell, Walter de la Mare and Louis MacNeice, and the actors John Gielgud and Edith Evans. Dylan, who was honoured to be on the organising committee, nevertheless turned up at the last minute, unsuitably dressed. While his performance went well, the dinner afterwards was a disaster. A woman was spotted roaring drunk in the ladies' cloakroom. 'That will be my wife,' Dylan mumbled. He was rude to T.S. Eliot and Caitlin suggested that a close friend of the distinguished poet and publisher lick off some ice cream that she had spilt on her arm. Sitwell was concerned. 'I am *worried* to think how his friends will be driven away if she goes on like that. He is such a wonderful poet – a really *great* one, and has very *endearing* qualities as a person.'

Sitwell's concern was well founded – and prophetic. Some of Dylan's old friends were finding Caitlin difficult to get on with. Gwen Watkins, always forthright, described her as 'the incarnation of suppressed rage'. She and Vernon were now living in a tiny flat in the Swansea suburb of Uplands with their baby, Rhiannon, but according to Gwen, Caitlin was clearly bored and showed no interest in them on the one occasion she and Dylan came to stay. There were the usual squabbles, and while Dylan never lost his temper with her, Caitlin could be very vindictive. Echoing the words that Dan had used to describe Dylan's father in the class-room, Gwen said: 'Being with her was rather like being in the same room with a tiger which was not very strongly chained'.

In April 1946 Dylan had written to Vernon from Holywell after a long silence. Vernon's second book of poems, *The Lamp and the Veil*, had been published the year before, but it received no acknowledgement from his friend. Dylan wrote now to ask to borrow an essay that Vernon had written on Wilfred Owen in connection with a BBC programme he was producing on the First World War poet, promising to return it 'spotless and unAeronwied'. He was clearly feeling the distance that had opened up between him and his hometown. 'It's strange to think of you, and Fred, and Tom sometimes, in Swansea again,' the letter said. Poking fun at Fred's painstaking working methods, he added: 'How is that blizzardly painter, that lightning artist, that prodigal canvas stacker? Has he reached the next finbone of the fish he was dashing off before the war? Please give him my love.' Dylan planned to visit his mother, who had been very ill, in Carmarthenshire and asked Vernon if he could stay in Swansea on the way back. 'Have you a little sheetless, must be sheetless, dog box for me to sleep in … Then we could, maybe, all spend one evening together, wipey eyed, remembering, locked in these damned days, the as-then-still-forgiven past.' Gwen felt Dylan was at his best on his home turf and without his wife. 'He was relaxed and appreciative, not needing to show off, eagerly listening to his friends' talk, laughing hilariously…' On one visit he joined Fred and Mary at the Watkinses' home, where he offered to read them something he was working on. Fred looked apprehensive because, Gwen suspected, he thought it was going to be a long poem. But it was an early draft of one of Dylan's broadcasts, probably 'Holiday Memory', a story about an August bank holiday on the beach, which is as fresh today as it seemed to Gwen then. She had never heard Dylan read before and was mesmerised by his voice and the descriptive humour of the piece, which he later read on the radio.

There was cricket on the sand, and sand in the sponge cake, sandflies in the watercress and foolish, mulish, religious donkeys on the unwilling trot. Girls undressed in slipping tents of propriety; under invisible umbrellas stout ladies dressed for the male and immoral sea. Little naked navvies dug canals; children with spades and no ambition built fleeting castles; wispy young men, outside the bathing huts, whistled at substantial young women and dogs who desired thrown stones more than the bones of elephants.

If Caitlin was around, Dylan's visits to Swansea were often a different story. Ethel Ross, Fred's sister-in-law, believed that the old gang bored his wife to death. Charades were a popular party game, especially among the Little Theatre crowd, and after a few rounds one evening Dylan donned a red scarf around his neck and pretended to be a gypsy, immediately capturing everyone's attention. 'It was remarkable,' Ethel said. 'He would enter completely into what he was doing and had enormous power over people.' After a few minutes, Caitlin stalked out, followed by an apologetic Dylan. It was just the kind of attention Caitlin the dancer wanted for herself, but Dylan was so much better at attracting it.

Early the following year, Dylan's bout of nostalgia prompted another return to Swansea to research a play for voices that is thought by many to be one of his finest works – *Return Journey*, an elegy to his young self and his hometown. It was a bitterly cold February and the ruined town was covered with snow in one of the harshest winters for years, but Dylan, assuming his old reporter's mantle, spent two days talking to Fred, Vernon and Dan, obtaining official records of all the shops that had been destroyed in the blitz, and discovering the extent of the damage to his old school. The drama, broadcast in the summer of 1947, is narrated by Dylan, who plays a character in search of 'Young Thomas', i.e. himself. As he wanders around the town, enquiring in pubs and talking to familiar-seeming faces, he creates vivid, tender snapshots of his childhood and days on the *Evening Post* that are full of self-deprecating humour. Young Thomas was 'a bombastic provincial Bohemian … a gabbing, ambitious, mock-tough, pretentious young man; and mole-y too…'. The final scene takes place in Cwmdonkin Park, where the park keeper finally settles the question of what happened to the lad.

Narrator
We had reached the last gate. Dusk grew around us and the town. I said: What has become of him now?

Park Keeper
Dead.

Narrator
The Park keeper said: *(The park bell rings)*

Park Keeper
Dead … Dead … Dead … Dead … Dead … Dead.

Return Journey's producer was Philip Burton, a former teacher from Port Talbot, a town to the east of Swansea that housed one of the largest steel works in Europe and a massive chemical plant. He was the legal guardian of Richard Burton, a former pupil and the twelfth of thirteen children, whose mother had died soon after her last baby was born. The boy, born Richard Jenkins, had been brought up by his aunt, but the schoolteacher nurtured his love of English – poetry in particular – and acting ability, helping him get a place at Oxford University by becoming his guardian. Burton's great love was Dylan Thomas – not just for their shared love of smoking, drinking and crosswords. They would soon meet and become friends while taking part in the same radio broadcast. In a few years Burton's readings of his hero's work would become as familiar as the poet's own.

When Dylan had finished the script it was too short. Philip Burton invited him to come and stay with him to work on it. He laid on a supply of Guinness, Dylan's preferred tipple at that time, and was surprised that he did not touch a drop during the whole ten-day period. 'This story about the old drunk didn't work at all … He was marvellous to work with. He was so different when he was alone … There was this frightful conflict between the poet and the performer. And if a third person walked into the room, the poet was pushed into a corner and the performer stepped forward.' Dylan was grateful that the trip to Swansea had put him back in touch with Charlie Fisher, whose address he had lost (again) after bumping into him in London. He wrote, tongue in cheek, with news of their mutual friends. 'Fred, I was astounded to see, was painting a rather careful picture of two herrings; Vernon, you would never believe, was writing a poem about spiritual essences.'

Sketch for a portrait of Professor Rowe by Alfred Hayes, 1923

Sketch for a portrait of Daniel Jones by Alfred Janes, 1947

CHAPTER TEN

AFTER THE FIGHT

Dylan had a few months' respite from the daily grind of austerity Britain and was not around to hear the broadcast of *Return Journey* in June. Thanks to Edith Sitwell's motherly concern about his lifestyle, he won a travelling scholarship to Italy worth £150 (about half the average salary) from the Society of Authors, of which her brother Osbert was deputy chair, and where she was on the awards committee. Dylan set off with the children, Caitlin, her sister Brigit and her son as a companion for Llewelyn. The plan was to find a writer's retreat where he could relax and work in peace, without having to worry about where the next cheque was coming from – although their funds dwindled predictably fast. On his first visit abroad, they saw the sights in Rome and Florence, stayed in a village outside the latter, then spent the last few weeks of their four-month expedition on Elba, where Caitlin took a fancy to the proprietor of their pensione. When they left, it wasn't the last he would see of her. Dylan had written only one long poem during the whole four months, *In Country Sleep*, and left without paying the bill.

Their patron Margaret Taylor saw to it that the Thomases had somewhere to live on their return, funded by her private income. She also arranged for Llewelyn to go to Magdalen College School in Oxford. Caitlin's father had been at Magdalen College, and Dylan, in spite of his own lack of enthusiasm for school and academia (or perhaps because of it), was keen that his son should

127

get a good education. The family's new home was a cottage in South Leigh, a village about ten miles west of Oxford, which they rented from Margaret for £1 a week. It had an outside toilet, no bathroom or electricity, but it was only a short train ride to London from the village railway station. 'I am so profoundly grateful to you,' Dylan wrote to Margaret. 'It means a heaven of a lot.'

The arrangement was a way of keeping Dylan close to Margaret, who was totally besotted with him, but at a distance from her husband. She made elaborate plans to elope with her poet and wrote to Dylan telling him that to go to bed with him would be like sleeping with a god. Neither proposition appealed. Caitlin discovered the letter and, while she was relieved that Dylan and Margaret were not lovers (and finding the god-like comparison risible), she was piqued enough to snip up and return a pretty petticoat that Margaret sent her as a peace offering. Caitlin regretted it later, because she rather liked the petticoat. Margaret even provided a gypsy caravan in the garden for Dylan to write in as a retreat from family life, but her tendency to pop in on him infuriated Caitlin: she was mindful never to disturb him when he was working, and wanted others to respect that rule. She tipped the caravan over. Margaret moved it further away. At least life, like the caravan, was back on a more even keel. Dylan found work again in the burgeoning post-war British film industry, which was boosted by a new tax on imported films. Gainsborough Studios was one of the UK companies desperate to find writers to satisfy the public's appetite for light relief in dreary times, and they offered Dylan a contract for £1,000 per script.

Another attraction of living in Oxfordshire was that Mervyn Levy was not far away. He was now heading up the art department at Chiseldon Army College near Swindon, which retrained demobbed soldiers. One of his staff members was a 'teenage surrealist', an untrained artist called Desmond Morris, who would later become an eminent zoologist and popular TV broadcaster and writer. He had been conscripted in 1946 – there was plenty of work getting the country back on its feet again – but hated the army and was lucky enough to be transferred to Chiseldon, and taken under Mervyn's wing. His brilliant Groucho Marx impersonation in particular, appealed hugely to Morris's surrealist tendencies. 'His art was quite traditional but he was so funny and outrageous,' Morris says. 'He lit up my life. Even my mother loved him because he was so outlandish.' On one occasion they were on a train journey when Mervyn instructed Morris to take out his portable typewriter and started walking up and down the carriage dictating a nonsensical letter in a very loud voice, which Morris pretended to take down.

Mervyn was living in a cottage on an estate owned by a wealthy art lover with whom he had served in the army, and as Dylan and Caitlin's cottage at South Leigh was in striking distance, they were able to visit. Mervyn persuaded Dylan to write an introduction to an exhibition that he held in March 1948 in Swindon – in all likelihood, given the corny prose, cooked up between them after a few drinks.

Morris admired Dylan's poetry and was delighted to be invited to meet him one Sunday, but was dismayed to find he was not at his best the day after one of the art lover's lavish Saturday night parties. He had got so drunk the night before that he had wet the bed, and much to Mervyn's dismay had ruined the mattress. On noticing one of Desmond's paintings he launched into a tirade about how hard it was to survive as a poet. 'Now look at that,' he boomed, 'you can sell that, can't you? The painter makes an object that can be sold. But not the poet.' He took a scribbled poem he was working on and slapped it on to the wall, holding it there as if it were a picture. 'Now I can't sell that, can I? No one would buy that bit of paper, would they?' Morris wished later that he had challenged him and bought it on the spot, or swapped it for a painting.

AN INTRODUCTION TO THE DRAWINGS
OF MERVYN LEVY

*

MERVYN LEVY, who happened to care about the purposes and
shapes of people quite a long time ago—he was born in
1914 and started drawing soon afterwards—has worked in
line and chalk, and brush and wash, with a passion that
makes his figures, his women, men, breasts, characters,
movement, substantial, sensual and delicate.

Red chalk glows in his drawings because his passion' for
the human figure is glowing.

His line is a line of love.

Ridicule and adoration are two sides of a method of praise.
Broad and precise, academically correct, and free from all
academic primness, these vigorous and subtle figures, squat,
sad, lustful, mocking, and acceptive, make an indispensable
world, in which the watcher, the witness, lives as exultantly
as the maker.

DYLAN THOMAS

WITNEY, OXON.
MARCH, 1948

*Dylan's introduction to the catalogue of
an exhibition by Mervyn Levy in 1948*

The conversation was disappointingly trivial, but then Dylan
stunned nineteen-year-old Morris with an impromptu pastiche of
the Lord's Prayer. He made it up on the spot as a tribute to a very
small man he had met the night before, who had made quite an

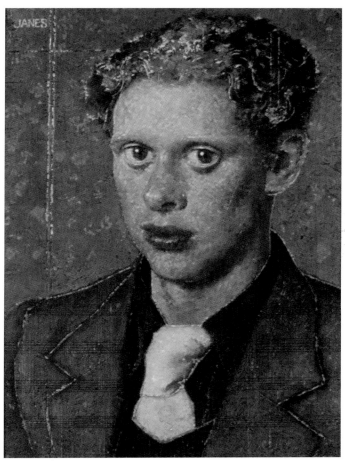

Dylan Thomas, 1934

'A frog in his salad days' is how Dylan Thomas later described this portrait by Janes, painted in their shambolic digs in 1934.

Mervyn Levy, 1931

This 1931 portrait of his fellow Swansea art student helped Janes win a scholarship in portraiture to the Royal Academy of Art.

National Library of Wales
© estate of the artist

Mervyn Levy, 1935

Janes painted this portrait of Levy in 1935 when they were sharing London digs with Thomas. 'Mervyn knew how to sit but Dylan was in and out like a cat in a tripe shop.'

City & Council of Swansea: Glynn Vivian Art Gallery Collection © estate of the artist

Fish and Pineapple, 1936

Janes worked meticulously on works like Fish and Pineapple. 'How is that blizzardly painter, that lightning artist, that prodigal canvas stacker?' Thomas joked later. 'Has he reached the next finbone of the fish he was dashing off before the war? Please give him my love.'

Private collection © estate of the artist

Still Life with Hyacinths, 1937

'His studio high above a flower shop near Swansea station could only be reached by climbing a stair which held every variety of smell from the flowers to the pickled objects he painted, fish, fruit and lobsters…' wrote Janes's friend the poet Vernon Watkins.

City & Council of Swansea: Glynn Vivian Art Gallery Collection © estate of the artist

Salome, 1938

This interpretation of the biblical story took Janes the whole of 1938 to paint.

The Queue, 1939

This was the last work that Janes painted until the end of the Second World War in 1945.

Private collection © estate of the artist

Castle Street Swansea after the Blitz, 1947

The building in the foreground is the bombed Kardomah Cafe, where Janes, Thomas and their friends used to meet to 'drink coffee dashes and argue the toss'.

Private collection © estate of the artist

Vernon Watkins, 1947

Janes considered this 1947 portrait of the poet Vernon Watkins to be one of his best.

Bank Holiday, 1953

Janes's scenes of everyday life with a surreal, satirical edge such as Bank Holiday, echoed short stories by Thomas like 'Holiday Memory': 'The sticks of rock, that we all sucked, were like barber's poles made of rhubarb.'

Dylan Thomas, 1953

This 1953 portrait of Thomas had to be finished from studies,
as the poet died before Janes could finish it.

Chirrup and Fruit, 1959

The title of this 1959 work is taken from 'Prologue', one of Janes's favourite poems by Thomas.

City & Council of Swansea: Glynn Vivian Art Gallery Collection © estate of the artist

Music of Colours – White Blossom, Ceri Richards, 1968

Richards, also from Swansea, produced many works inspired by Thomas and their mutual friend Vernon Watkins, who had written a poem with this title.

City & Council of Swansea: Glynn Vivian Art Gallery Collection © Ceri Richards 2004. All rights reserved, DACS

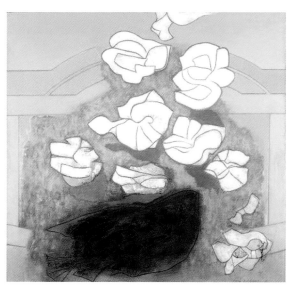

impression on him. 'Our midget which art in heaven, miniature be thy name...' he intoned, using a boiled potato on a fork as a microphone, and continued with dazzling wordplay until the end: 'For ever and ever, Tom Thumb.'

Mervyn later took up a post as a higher-education art teacher and lecturer in Bristol. One night he and the landlady of his digs were woken by furious battering at the door at 2.30 a.m. It was Dylan. 'Mervy! Mervy!' he shouted. 'We've come to see you!' There was no question of staying at Mervyn's digs, but he managed to get Dylan and his travelling companion rooms in a nearby hotel. Dylan was clearly exhausted and after they had caught up on each other's news over a few bottles of beer, Dylan asked Mervyn to sing him to sleep with a favourite old song. Although he intended to go back to Oxford the next day, he spent three restful days with Mervyn, drinking very little, eating well and going to the cinema, where, Mervyn thought, he felt 'snug and safe'.

Two years after the war had ended, daily life was still a struggle, with rations of basic foodstuffs and clothes sometimes cut instead of increasing. During the freezing winter of 1947, even potatoes had not survived and were rationed for the first time since the outbreak of war. Luckily, the Janes household was receiving food parcels from the US, where Mary's sister Ethel, an unmarried school teacher who lived with the family, was on an exchange programme and had swapped places with her American counterpart. Mary's hitherto unpublished letters about life at home in Swansea offer a snapshot of how Fred, Dan and Vernon were readjusting to domesticity and trying to regain a foothold in their respective fields. There was also occasional news of Dylan. He wrote to Vernon to tell him about an invitation from the British Council to visit Paris. 'We are staying, for no reason, at the Hungarian embassy. Or perhaps I am someone else.' The prospect amused his friends but the visit was cancelled. Dylan's third anthology in the US, *Selected Writings*, had been published in 1946 and from across the Atlantic, Ethel gave news of his growing reputation, posting home articles and poems about and by him that appeared in prestigious publications like the *New York Times*, *Atlantic Monthly* and *Time* magazine. According to artists she met, he was already a by-word in Greenwich Village. Her parcels of food, clothes for four-year-old Ross, perfume and nylons for Mary and even linseed oil for Fred's paint were very welcome. 'Things are so tight now that we do not eat any meals without some dish or ingredient from America,' Mary wrote. The goodies received by their American guest were an added bonus. 'Don't tell,' Fred wrote to Ethel, 'but we have done quite well recently; I believe I have actually gained a little weight.' To celebrate their wedding anniversary, Fred opened a bottle of whisky that the exchange teacher had brought back from a trip to Scotland. 'Just a sip mind you – we're keeping the rest for Christmas.' He was particularly vexed when petrol rations were cut altogether in the autumn of 1947, as they had mortgaged a rental property his mother owned to buy a car the day before – something he couldn't bear to be without. The local medical fraternity still managed to organise a good Hospital Ball, however – a dinner dance with duck and ice cream for 150 guests, and plenty of gin brought by the doctors, who scorned the beer provided. Mary stuck to sherry and was spared the hangover that afflicted some others, including Fred, who was 'roaring'.

Ethel also wrote tantalisingly of the modern art collections and exhibitions she saw in New York, sending catalogues home for her brother-in-law. 'How much better it would be if you had been here instead of me. There are so many first rate exhibitions that you would revel in.' Fred now had a part-time teaching job at the art school in Swansea and was trying out new painting techniques, mainly with still lifes and flower pictures in a room at his mother's house, selling work privately and exhibiting where he could – there were no commercial galleries in Swansea. The Contemporary Art Society for Wales had bought *Salome*, the painting which had taken him a year to complete, but when he and Mary made a trip to see it in Cyfarthfa Castle Museum in Merthyr Tydfil, they found it in a cupboard. Fred didn't just hit the roof, Mary wrote, 'the roof's off!!'.

He also tried his hand at portraiture again, capturing Dan's penetrating intelligence, his composer's pencil tucked into his jacket pocket, and in gentle blues and greys, Vernon's ethereal otherworldliness. Fred thought it was the most interesting portrait he had painted so far. Perhaps prompted by Dylan's *Return Journey* he painted the only street scene of his career – a picture of the bombed-out Kardomah building.

In 1947 Fred took part in a London show of Welsh painting at the St George Gallery in Grosvenor Street, and the portrait of Vernon and a still life, *Little Cactus*, were shown at a mixed show at Heal's department store, which Fred thought 'lousy'. His plan was to work towards a one-man show rather than exhibiting in dribs and drabs and he hankered after moving back to the capital – or even to America – wondering about buying a big house in Hampstead and dividing it into flats to rent. 'Fred feels he should be there to get on, keeping contact with galleries. I think we would have a more stimulating time on the whole. It is really dead here, the same old round & crowd and the deadness of blitzed Swansea,' Mary confided in Ethel. He had to make do with a visit to Charlie Fisher in the meantime to see the 'absolutely magnificent' Van Gogh exhibition at the Tate (now Tate Britain). Charlie, who was now on the staff at Reuters news agency, took Fred into the office. 'He said it was like a mad house,' Mary wrote, 'a hundred typewriters and papers flying and telephones going – just like the movies'.

There were a few cultural offerings in Swansea – the Little Theatre was still going strong, despite the difficulty of finding premises in the semi-derelict town. Mary confessed that she found rehearsals for a production of Vernon's *The Ballad of the Mari Lwyd* pretty hard going. Visiting him in Pennard, where he and Gwen had moved to a remote wooden bungalow on the cliffs overlooking the Bristol Channel, was much more fun. Fred and Mary liked the couple enormously, and found their battles and arguments very amusing. Gwen had married very young and although motherhood was her priority, life could be frustrating in the sticks with a husband who came home from work and wrote poetry in the evenings. Like many couples at the time, they had no car, telephone or washing machine to help with the nappies, and Gwen often just had books for company. It was just as well she loved reading.

One afternoon, Vernon had his guests in fits by reading out some of Dylan's old letters, one of which asked for a loan to fund the return of a book he had borrowed from Vernon.

> I hate having to ask you Vernon and will not attempt to describe how grateful I am to you, but the weasels take their hats off to me as I slink by. I have nearly finished my novel and when it is reviewed the critics will describe me as the bully busting Thomas, the Rimbaud of Cwmdonkin Drive.

The novel, *Adventures in the Skin Trade*, was never finished, although it became the title of a future collection of short stories, but the epithet stuck.

Vernon, like Dylan, was finding an audience for his work in the US, and in March 1948 he showed the visitors a copy of *Poetry* magazine which had used Fred's portrait of him to illustrate one of his poems. The Watkinses now had a little girl, a playmate for

Ross, and Fred became godfather to their first son, Gareth, at his christening in 1948. 'Vernon got a wonderful white cake and a bottle of wine, and everything was done in style,' Mary wrote. Gwen, who originally came from Bournemouth, was enjoying discovering the Gower peninsula – as she wrote to Ethel. 'Pennard is so wonderful that we can have no regrets for the town. Bishopston Valley is full of white violets and primroses, and the bays are incredibly beautiful.'

Dan Jones was back too, living with his new wife and their baby, whom they named after Dylan. 'Dan is still spreading himself and Irene and Dylan II over the vast expanse of their single room in Mumbles before moving to a house,' Fred wrote to Ethel. The single room was a step up – Dan and Irene lived at first in an old bus parked just above Mumbles Head. On hot days the postman was surprised to find Dan working in almost nothing but a green eyeshade. They also spent a lot of time in the White Rose pub, Fred wrote. 'Dan composes furiously and drinks furiouslyer [sic]. I've had to give up these sessions. They are too expensive.' The first live performance of one of Dan's orchestral works didn't enthuse Mary, however. 'Sometimes, between ourselves,' she confided to Ethel, 'I wonder if I am in the midst of a few near misses'.

The lot of a housewife and mother in post-war Britain, especially when married to someone who lived for his art, was beginning to take its toll on Mary as well as Gwen. Her awareness of how different life could be in the US, via Ethel's letters and their American guest, only increased her frustration.

Margaret is constantly staggered at the way women put up with everything and are expected to drudge and economise and go without. Fred, I don't think, is keen to go anywhere but nearer London. He would rather die in Britain etc. Well he's got the supreme spiritual satisfaction of the creative worker. He has started a portrait of me (not I hasten to assure you that I as the mere subject am of the slightest importance. Never forget that a work of art lives irrespective of its subject. It's the way it's painted, gentleman, that counts). Then why not paint the kitchen stove & save me the wear and tear of rushing to sittings?

When he finished the portrait, she was shocked that Fred had changed the colour of her clothes to green and yellow. 'You've made me look like a ruddy daffodil!' she protested.

Life for Dylan and Caitlin in Oxfordshire was a little easier. Dylan's film work and growing audience in the US was bringing in more money, but it soon disappeared on lavish treats in London and paying off debts – including £85 to the tax authorities, who had caught up with him. He joined the National Liberal Club – which he christened the National Lavatory on account of the peer who used to pop in to use the facilities – but left it for the Savage, which had an artier clientele. The turnaround in his fortunes was short lived. The government abolished the import tax on films a year later, not too long after the studios folded and none of the scripts that Dylan was working on went into production. He had, meanwhile, written no poetry and turned down offers of work from the BBC.

Little of the money that Dylan earned was given to Caitlin for housekeeping. Life was a grind for her in South Leigh, relieved only by visits to the pub or the odd trip to Oxford or London. Dylan's announcement that D.J. and Florence, who had broken her leg and was confined to bed, were coming to stay in a cottage at the other end of the village, showed his sense of responsibility to his parents (his sister Nancy had fallen for an RAF pilot during the war and remarried), but only added to Caitlin's load and sense of isolation. A daily help was hired but that was not enough to pacify her. As she said herself, with no skill or the chance to find a rich lover, she was stuck. 'Sometimes he [Dylan] would go off in the mornings and then not return at night, and I would be raging by the time he did come home,' she wrote, regretting the effect on Llewelyn, who was old enough to understand what was going on, and acknowledging that there was little in the way of home comfort to keep Dylan there anyway. When Caitlin took the children away for a brief summer break, leaving Dylan in South Leigh with his elderly parents and nosy Margaret, a letter from him to her acknowledged that he found the circumstances just as trying and spent as much time as possible in the bedroom writing letters. It expressed, as his letters to Caitlin always did, his devotion and longing.

When Dylan had been researching *Return Journey* he had talked to Philip Burton about returning to Laugharne and in October 1948, barely a year after moving to South Leigh, he started to make inquiries about the possibility of renting a house there. 'Here I am too near London,' he wrote to friends in the town. 'I undertake all sorts of little jobs, broadcasting etc, which hinder my own work. In Laugharne if I could live there, I would work half the year on my film scripts and half on my own poems and stories: cutting out all time wasting broadcasts, articles, useless London visits.'

Margaret took it upon herself to look for a property, spurred on by Dylan fantasising about what life would be like back in the town. She found a house on stilts with a wooden verandah nestling above the Taf estuary, the Boat House, reached by steep steps leading down from the cliff path, and took out a lease on it. It had no running water or electricity but the capable benefactor soon saw to that, as well as finding a cottage, Pelican House, opposite Brown's Hotel for D.J. and Florence. Llewelyn was left behind to board at Magdalen College School, but in May 1949 a new life at the Boat House was about to begin for the rest of the family, with a new baby, too. Colm Garan (Welsh for 'heron') arrived on 24 July.

The Boat House in Laugharne, Thomas's
'seashaken house on a breakneck of rocks'

CHAPTER ELEVEN

THE SEASHAKEN HOUSE

Back in Laugharne, Dylan soon fell into a routine that would enable him to focus on writing poetry again. Mornings were spent reading, then he would go the Pelican, as everyone called it, to see his parents, read his work in progress to his father and do the *Times* crossword. Sometimes he would work there too, to get away from the children. After a couple of beers at Brown's Hotel and a chinwag with Ivy Williams, who knew everything about the latest goings on in Laugharne, he would go home for a lunch that often consisted of flat fish and cockles gathered from the sand in the estuary. Caitlin had learned about 'treading' from the locals, a method of catching fish that burrowed in the sand by feeling them with your feet and flicking them out. Dylan's afternoons were spent writing in a disused garage along the cliff path that he had adopted as a study. He lined the walls with reproductions of pictures and photographs – including of Edith Sitwell – that Caitlin cut out of magazines and in winter months Caitlin would light the anthracite stove in the mornings to warm it up.

Their daughter Aeron was by now old enough to form her own memories of life in the Boat House, which she recorded in a memoir, *My Father's Places*. 'My mother was the mother and the father of the whole outfit. She looked after us all and treated my father as a further child, organised his day for him, would even wash him and bathe him, do everything for him.' Sometimes she even locked him in the shed until it was time to collect him in the early evening.

Mother would organise his work day. Between 2 p.m. and 6 p.m. he had to work on his poetry, and she would send him off to the shed. We would be told not to make a noise if we went past it. One day I organised a tribe of Indians with the local children and the dog, Mabley, a very hysterical dog whom we excited into a frenzy and then passed the shed with our bicycle bells going at full tilt.

Her reward was a beating with a brush by Caitlin in the evening. Physical punishment by Dylan was unthinkable. In the evening he returned to the Boat House, where Caitlin would run him a weekly bath and lay across the tub on the soap tray saucers of sweets and savoury snacks, with a bottle of fizzy pop to wash them down. After supper they would go to the pub together, leaving Aeron in charge of baby Colm, returning at around 10 p.m. and going to bed. At weekends friends might come back with them to party and watch Caitlin dance in one of her twirling skirts to records on the gramophone.

Dylan's weekly bath night was very special for Aeron because afterwards he would sometimes read to her from *Grimm's Fairy Tales*. He was a loving father, but today's notions of parenting and quality time were unheard of in his generation. It was the woman's job to look after the children. Story time with Dylan was very precious and rolling favourite words around their mouths like 'Rumpelstiltskin' and 'Struwwelpeter' tasted as sweet as a gobstopper. Dylan even rearranged all the furniture in the living room so that they could pretend it was the witch's house in *Hansel and Gretel*. He would always buy books for the children when he could afford it, and Aeron's disappointment at *The Wind in the Willows* being the only present she received one Christmas vanished when she realised that Dylan would read it to her himself. His hysterical, high-pitched Toad and the naughty weasels were favourite characters. Constant intellectual stimulation was provided by visits from artistic and literary friends like Fred, Mervyn and Vernon. Augustus John stayed at the Boat House and painted Dylan several times. As Dylan's fame grew, academics and students were all made welcome. One day at school the feisty Aeron was introduced to an inspector as Dylan Thomas's daughter. 'I'm Aeron Thomas,' she corrected, full of indignation. 'Dylan Thomas's daughter is not a name.' Dylan's heartfelt letter of thanks to Margaret Taylor for her generosity and effort on his behalf in buying the Boat House 'in face of callous & ungrateful behaviour' expresses his relief at being back 'in this place I love and where I want to live and where I can work and where I have started work (my own) already…'. Within weeks he had written 'Over Sir John's Hill', a striking and powerful poem rich with the images of the Taf estuary that he saw every day, but preoccupied with death and the loss of innocence. It was the first of the handful of more measured and mellow poems that he composed in Laugharne.

Later that month a letter arrived at the Boat House from America. Dylan had been trying to fix a visit there for years, not just to the land of cowboys, Indians and the Marx Brothers, but keen to earn money on the lecture circuit and promote sales of US editions of his books to his growing audience there. In Britain, a new pared-down kind of poetry, known as The Movement, that rejected the lyric romanticism of some of his work was more in tune with the times. Among younger English writers, Philip Larkin, now a librarian, had changed his favourable view since hearing Dylan read at Oxford, and his friend Kingsley Amis, who was soon to take up a post lecturing at Swansea University, poured scorn on his work.

The letter was from John Malcolm Brinnin, a man who would wield enormous influence on Dylan's reputation and, when he later published his account of their relationship in *Dylan Thomas in America*, not always for the better. A lecturer and writer, he was also the ambitious young director of the Poetry Centre of the Young Men's and Young Women's Hebrew Association (YM-YWHA) in New York, and invited Dylan to come and read there for a fee of $500 (£1 was worth almost $3 at the time). Dylan wasted little time in accepting the invitation, saying that he planned to go in January or February of the following year. There were other commitments to meet in the meantime. Dylan was still working for the BBC, travelling to London – a 500-mile round trip from Laugharne – or Cardiff and in October 1949 to its studios in Swansea to record a programme about the town with his old friends Fred, Vernon, Dan and John Prichard. All of them were by now growing in reputation, and the broadcast featured on the front cover of *Radio Times*.

Cover of Radio Times, *October 1949 featuring the BBC's*
'Swansea and the Arts' radio broadcast.
Seated from left: Vernon Watkins, John Prichard, Alfred
Janes, Daniel Jones, Dylan Thomas

As well as exhibiting work in the important Redfern Gallery in Mayfair in London the year before, Fred achieved his goal of a one-man show that year of forty paintings at the Glynn Vivian Art Gallery in Swansea, which included his portraits of Dan and Vernon. Dan's First Symphony was to be played by the London Philharmonic Orchestra at the town's music festival and Vernon's third book of poems, *The Lamp and the Veil*, had been published in 1945 (Dylan had inevitably left the copy Vernon sent him in a taxi). Their friend John Prichard had won the prestigious *Atlantic* Prize, awarded by the magazine for short stories, and was writing his first novel, *A Journey to the End of the Alphabet*, which would be published two years later. For the broadcast, each would read from his own script, with Dylan as the link man.

Making much play on the fact that the studios were situated in a road called The Grove, Dylan conjured up images of the group as former creatures from classical mythology. 'Five of us then, sit in this desecrated Grove, on chairs, not hillocks; our little cloven feet are shoed; our shirt cuffs fray where flowery bangles once budded; some of us wear glasses; and the mead is off.' The point was to explain why they had all chosen to live and work in Swansea – although Dylan excused himself for living in Carmarthenshire with 'I am a globetrotter, I live in the next county'. After a blisteringly witty diatribe against artists from Wales who settled in London but tried not to be Welsh – 'Ektually,' they say, 'I was born in Cwmbwrla, but Soho's better for my gouaches' – he introduced each of his companions by turn. Vernon he described as 'the most profound and greatly accomplished Welshman writing poems in English'.

John, who was now a civil servant, was praised for writing stories 'full of the smell and feel of everyday dark talk' that wryly opened windows on the town. He was the only one to make the observation that their generation was the first to be brought up speaking only English, despite the fact that they had either one or two parents who were Welsh speaking – the language of miners and farmers, not the educated middle class. It was strange, he said, not to understand the language that you heard at home and on the streets of your hometown. He wondered if this, combined with being the first generation that had grown up listening to the radio, had given them a particular sensitivity to English. Vernon's contribution emphasised the lively nature of arts in the town, and its lack of pretension. To be pompous in Swansea, he said, was also to be ludicrous. He highlighted its extraordinary and contradictory setting – the docks, the sea, the town with its almost vertical hills, but the secret landscapes of Gower on its doorstep.

Fred too emphasised the town's conflicts and contradictions – the dereliction of Landore, site of the town's first copper works and one of the world's largest steel works, in contrast with the awe-inspiring beauty of Rhossili; coal trimming alongside county cricket. They stimulated his mind, and kept 'his imagination in good fettle'. While he felt that Swansea offered enough kindred spirits to provide an essential exchange of ideas, he also pointed out that painters, unlike musicians and poets who can listen to recordings and read books, can only study the works of masters past and present in national art collections, which were always in big cities. London, it seemed, was still calling Fred.

This is how Dylan described him:

Years ago, when he was a student at the Royal Academy of Arts, I shared rooms (and what rooms) with Alfred Janes, painter, and those ginger bearded days seem full to me now, of his apples carved in oil, his sulphurously glowing lemons, his infernal kippers. Waking up, one saw all around one the Welsh fires burning behind those fanatically diligent, minutely life-cut, fossil-indented interlogical patterns of rind and scale, and felt like a fish on a red-hot flowery slab. After many Academy awards, and several paintings hung in London galleries, he returned to Swansea to work and experiment, which were synonymous. And a very strange world of enormous human (maybe) beings in flowing Renaissance gowns and herringbone tweeds, acting peculiar, sometimes levitating, in geometrical alle(maybe)gories came into existence in number 90 High Street.

Unable to resist the pun, Dylan described Dan Jones as 'a composer of music on a very great scale'. Dan was openly critical of the lack of opportunities in Swansea to play or listen to orchestral or chamber music, but argued that this mattered more to an instrumental player than to a composer, who could parcel up his scores and send them out into the world. After a fourteen-year absence, Swansea simply felt like home to Dan, and he felt he could do his best work there: 'Visual fascination and contrast; friendliness in the people; the comfort and stimulation of friendship; Swansea offers me all these things. No wonder that I feel happier and can work here better than anywhere else.'

Dylan Thomas in New York on the first of his US tours in 1950. He gave 40 readings in 90 days, travelling the length and breadth of the country

CHAPTER TWELVE

AMERICAN DREAM

Dylan would never be satisfied with a horizon that stretched only across the Bristol Channel. On the other side of the world plans were taking shape for his first tour of the US, where he was being fêted as the most influential young poet in England. Significant institutions like the Museum of Modern Art in New York and the Library of Congress in Washington were enquiring about bookings to Brinnin, who was now effectively acting as agent for Dylan, organising a tour of readings and talks for 15 per cent of his fees. With uncharacteristic financial acumen, Dylan pointed out he had no money and would need some on arrival, and that he would need to be paid travel expenses – a wise move as he had set his sights on a visit to California.

At first, the plan had been for Caitlin to come with him as a well-deserved break from the realities of life in Laugharne, which, financially at least, was not as productive as Dylan had hoped. His film work had dried up and so, once again, had the goodwill of the local tradespeople. The coal, essential for heating and hot water, had been cut off, the milk delivery was about to follow suit and there were other outstanding debts to pay. Cheques had been bouncing at the Savage Club and demands came from publishers who had paid advances but not received what they had commissioned. It was taking longer for Caitlin to recover from giving birth than before. With two small children to look after (Llewelyn was now boarding at Magdalen College School) she resented Dylan's trips away from Laugharne to work for the BBC, although apart from royalties, which were paid only twice a year, and fees for publishing the few poems he was managing to write, it was their only source of income. David Higham was always willing to negotiate advances against future income for Dylan – but he wisely never lent him any money.

Dylan decided that it would be impractical and unwise for Caitlin to accompany him, which only added to her resentment, but he placated her with promises of cheques that he would send back from what was shaping up to be a lucrative and totally unprecedented tour of the US by a British poet. He would be away for four months, and travel thousands of miles from New York to the west coast and back again via Canada and Florida, with thirty-five performances scheduled in ninety-seven days. It was like a rock star going on tour but with no support network of band members, roadies and personal assistants. Dylan was going it alone – but not before calling in on Dan. Sometimes he would even write notes to Dan in rhyme:

A bilingual lyric for DJ Jones

Aujourd'hui
I'll be
If je possibly can
Dans me Swansea
Avec me Dan

Now there was only time to send a brief telegram from the Boat House, asking Dan to meet him at a pub on his way to London to catch the flight to New York.

Dylan arrived at Idlewild airport on 21 February, armed with an anthology of modern British poets that he had chosen himself and written out longhand. Brinnin met him and spent a couple of days showing him the sights, introducing him to dingy Irish bars, where he seemed at ease, and to New York's literati at dinners and parties, where he didn't. Though Brinnin claimed that Dylan rarely ate a square meal, D.J. and Florence learned otherwise in a letter that listed what he had been feasting on, from huge milkshakes and T-bone steaks, to fried shrimp and chicken – a welcome change from post-war rations and Caitlin's Irish stews.

But as his first appearance drew near, Dylan became literally sick with nerves, vomiting up blood and claiming that he had cirrhosis of the liver. More than 1,000 tickets had been sold for the first of two readings at the YM-YWHA Poetry Centre, many of them for standing room only. In the dressing room beforehand he was overcome by a coughing fit so powerful that Brinnin had to help him stand upright. Then, as he had done so many times before, he regained his composure and read from poets including Yeats, Hardy, Lawrence, Auden, MacNeice and Sitwell, adding only a couple of his own poems at the end. His rich delivery and self-deprecating humour were a revelation to American audiences used to more sober, academic readings. There were standing ovations either side of the performance and he struggled to get out of the building through the crowd.

'I felt a very lonely foreign midget orating up there, in a huge hall, before all those faces,' he wrote to Caitlin soon after, adding, with typical modesty, 'but the readings went well'. His letter revealed that he was clearly overwhelmed not only by the sheer scale, density and loudness of New York, but by the prospect of the 'appallingly extensive' enterprise he had undertaken. The letter, like the others he wrote regularly to her, expressed his undying, insatiable love; the homesickness he felt for Laugharne, and how much he missed the children. He promised he would send home cheques, drink nothing but ice cold beer, and was taken aback by the amount of spirits that Americans drank – something he knew he had to avoid if he was to keep up the pace.

Brinnin chaperoned him at first around prestigious east coast universities like Columbia, Yale, Harvard, Cornell and Bryn Mawr, where his approach showed students that poetry, far from being a dry academic subject, could be enormously enjoyable, especially if they gathered around to hear him talk about it afterwards. Then he set off alone for the Midwest. Even for a restless man who was used to living out of a suitcase, making his own arrangements to travel around a strange continent, often on endless train journeys, and finding his way to venues in unfamiliar cities was daunting. Without Caitlin there to see to all his needs, just getting his laundry done was beyond him and looking smart often meant buying new shirts. Every two or three days would mean meeting new hosts, welcome committees, cocktail receptions, dinners and parties after his performances. Although his readings were as rapturously received as they had been in New York, the strain was enormous and Dylan's coping mechanism – drinking – especially in intimidating academic circles, risked damaging his already perilous state of health, not to mention his reputation.

As news of his antics filtered back to England, his friends became concerned. Vernon knew how important the US visit was to Dylan, both financially and to affirm his standing, but he above anyone knew how impossible it would be for him to write poetry with all the distractions of touring. He wrote to his own contacts in America, asking for news and suggesting that they try and get in touch with him. One anecdote told of how a poet and professor of history had presented Dylan with two copies of his own books, to be met with indifference. When it came to the third tome, *Conservatism Revisited*, Dylan replied: 'Better it should never have been visited at all.' A newspaper cutting was sent reporting Dylan as saying that Vernon was the best poet writing in English.

Another, from the poet Oscar Williams, said that his readings were magnificent and all America was in love with him.

From Berkeley near San Francisco he went to Vancouver, then back to the University of California in Los Angeles, where he had the telephone number of the English writer Christopher Isherwood, whose stories about life in pre-war Berlin inspired the Hollywood musical and film *Cabaret*. He had left the UK for the US before the war, and the two had never met. Isherwood offered to show Dylan the way from his hotel to the reading, which was preceded by a lunch with startled academics. The performance itself went down a lot better with the students than the staff. Two old cronies from his wartime scriptwriting days were also now in LA, and once back in the company of friends Dylan was able to relax. When they asked him what he would like to do, he said he would like to meet Charlie Chaplin – and a visit to his house, by which time the party was well oiled, was duly arranged. When Dylan asked his hero to send Caitlin a telegram saying they had met because otherwise she would never believe him, the good-natured Chaplin obliged. The evening ended in a bar, where someone said that Isherwood's book was not as good as his last one – for which Dylan attacked him.

The laid-back California lifestyle was so appealing that Dylan tried to cancel his next stop, Florida, claiming that he was ill. A more likely cause was an eighteen-year-old girl with a yellow sports car whom he had met on a second visit to San Francisco. Brinnin persuaded him just to postpone the visit to Florida, which was sandwiched between a quick stop in New York and another week of back-to-back readings in the Midwest. By the time Dylan returned to New York he was an A-list celebrity, and had rubbed shoulders (and possibly more) with several stars himself, including the glamorous Hollywood actress Shelley Winters. Eminent poets and writers like Henry Miller, E.E. Cummings and W.H. Auden had made his acquaintance, or listened to him read. He had never offered the same selection of poems twice and sometimes invented the programme as he went along, according to the audience's reaction – a true showman.

Caitlin expected her husband home in early May, but he wrote to say he would be delayed because he wanted to come home by boat. She had been surprised to receive more letters than she expected during his trip, but was rightly suspicious of his declarations of displeasure at being away from home and undying love. Many women found Dylan's combination of Bohemian poet and little boy lost irresistible and during the final two weeks of his tour he had a relationship with a young female poet, and juggled dalliances with a former model (who later denied an affair, saying she only wanted to be nice to him) and a serious young editor at *Harper's Bazaar* called Pearl Kazin, a graduate in English from Radcliffe, Harvard's college for women. Dylan boarded the *Queen Elizabeth* on 31 May laden with presents for himself and the family. A group of friends and admirers waved him off, including a tearful Pearl. It was not the last time she would cry over Dylan Thomas. And he had certainly not seen the last of John Malcolm Brinnin. After four months alone in Laugharne with the children, Caitlin was in the mood for the welcome-home celebrations that friends had organised in London. But she was disappointed to find that Dylan, who had clearly done enough partying to last a lifetime and had a racking cough, was exhausted and just wanted to go home. En route they stopped off in Swansea to visit the Watkins family at their clifftop bungalow. A lot of the old gang assembled to hear all about Dylan's adventures: Fred had given Caitlin and Dylan a lift along with Mary and Ross; Dan and Irene were there with their Dylan. It was a lovely summer's day and Vernon and Caitlin were keen to go for a swim, but when they all set off for the nearest sandy bay, Dylan soon got out of breath and couldn't carry on.

Caitlin, for once, was not the 'simmering cauldron of rage' familiar to Gwen and, invigorated by her very long swim, was happy to chat to the other wives. Dan and Dylan soon fell into their childhood routine, as Caitlin said they always did, and decided to re-enact a film about Egyptian tombs that had terrified them as children in the Uplands fleapit. Dylan played the Egyptologist while Vernon was the tomb robber, and Dan was the mummified pharaoh, posing in an old zinc bath that they turned upright and used as a tomb. They played cricket and had tea on rugs on the lawn, with sandwiches and cakes made by Gwen. Ethel Ross, Fred's sister-in-law, arrived and noted Dylan's new look.

He was wearing American clothes: low waisted trousers, a drip dry button-through shirt which kept popping open out above his navel as he lolled about waiting to bat. Cait was wearing a patterned peasant skirt. As he went into bat she ran and put her arms around him. 'Not here in front of these people Cait', he said softly. The light vanished from her face as she turned to stare at us.

Ethel had noticed that Caitlin kept her distance. 'I don't think Caitlin was particularly friendly or forthcoming when we were about. We weren't really her cup of tea.'

The grammar school boys were all family men now, busy earning a living through their artistic output, and in Fred's case part-time teaching. Vernon still had his day job in the bank. Dylan's visit to the US was not to be his last, and while he would still pass through Swansea – it was the end of the railway line to London – this was the last time that they would all be together. Gwen described it 'one of the great lost days', but Ethel struck a more chilling note. The Cold War between the Soviet Union and the West had taken a sinister turn a few months before Dylan's arrival with the announcement by Senator Joseph McCarthy that the US State Department had been infiltrated by communists, who would be rooted out. The era of McCarthyism, with its pillorying of many people in public life before official tribunals, created fear and paranoia, especially among the liberal establishment. Dylan spoke despairingly of the witch hunt and said he was sure McCarthyism would triumph. Ethel, who was well aware of the conflict it was creating in the US, said that if she thought that, she would take a dose of Luminal. Dylan stared at her for a long time and then smiled. 'Lovely stuff, Luminal, gives lovely, lovely dreams.' Ethel was shocked. Luminal was a powerful sedative that could be fatal in an overdose.

If Dylan had written to Caitlin more often than she expected while he was away, the lack of promised cheques was less surprising. Dylan had earned $7,800 on tour (about £2,600), but almost half went on his travel expenses, Brinnin's share and US tax. The $4,000 that was left was a decent income by any standards, but Dylan claimed he returned with only about $200. Brinnin, familiar by now with the way that money slipped through Dylan's fingers, had thoughtfully tucked $800 into a beautiful handbag that he sent back for Caitlin as a gift. But nothing would compensate for her discovery of letters that Dylan had carelessly left in a jacket pocket. They were from his *Harper's Bazaar* squeeze Pearl Kazin, addressed to Dylan at the Savage Club, where he had been staying while trying to re-establish his BBC contacts and find more work. Caitlin, who was already pregnant for the fourth time, was livid, but when Dylan dismissed Pearl as just another of his 'ardents', his term for the eager young women who hung around after his readings, she believed him. A stinging rebuke that she sent to Pearl helped vent her rage. In any case, she put such infidelities down to Dylan's basic need for drunken sex, a bed for the night, hot drinks and a cuddle when he was away from home. He was after all, as she said, very 'cuddlesome'.

Brinnin discovered for himself what Dylan was spending his money on when he visited London in the autumn, where he was greeted by the poet in smart new clothes, the ubiquitous Woodbine cigarette now replaced by a huge cigar. Dylan was eager to return the hospitality he had been offered in New York, and a round of literary parties, dinners, visits to the theatre and a tour of Dylan's favourite drinking holes followed. At the seedy Mandrake in Soho, the American was bemused that no one paid any attention to Dylan at all, until it was pointed out that this was actually a sign of deference.

Dylan had a brief affair with Pearl Kazin, an American journalist. She came to see him in London where they were photographed together by John Malcolm Brinnin, Dylan's US tour manager

Another transatlantic visitor soon arrived in London – Pearl. When the three met for drinks it was clear to Brinnin that the affair was serious, and there was desperation in Dylan's voice when he revealed as much. 'I'm in love with Pearl, and I'm in love with my wife,' he confessed. 'I don't know what to do.' His anxiety was relieved in the short term by Pearl's departure for France, but matters were soon taken out of his hands by the ever-solicitous Margaret Taylor, who was now living in London. She had suspected what was going on and intercepted the lovers' messages at the Savage Club. Whether out of spite, jealousy or consideration for Caitlin, she got straight on the train to Carmarthen to tell her all about the smart, efficient young editor who her husband was having an affair with.

If she had been furious before, Caitlin's feelings towards Pearl were now murderous. It was deeply humiliating to discover that her husband had been taking Pearl around his London haunts and even on a weekend to Brighton while she was stuck in Laugharne with the children. When Dylan arrived back at the Boat House and she confronted him, he tried to talk his way out of her accusations, and in desperation attempted to persuade one of her close friends that Margaret, 'the grey fiend', had made the whole thing up. The row that night was vicious and the first of what were now violent confrontations, usually after a drinking session at Brown's Hotel, in which Caitlin would physically attack Dylan, sometimes knocking him unconscious by banging his head on the floor.

Aeron was used to her mother's temper, and with her slight frame and curly hair she looked so like her father she was often the butt of it. But she could always escape to Granny's house for a cuddle. Florence was careful not to take sides. 'I'll tell Daddy you are here to look after me,' she would say. 'She's got a terrible temper, she can't help it.' But when Aeron asked why she couldn't call someone a bastard, or say 'for Christ's sake' or 'fuck you' as her mother did, Florence put her right. But Aeronwy was old enough now to notice that the atmosphere at home had turned decidedly cold, as Dylan slunk around the house like Mabley the dog when he was in disgrace.

One night Caitlin was so angry that she tore up the final manuscript of the poem he was working on, 'In the White Giant's Thigh'. In her hormonal pregnant state, its sexual imagery upset her so much that she threw the pieces out of the window on to the mud flats below. When she woke early the next morning, full of contrition in her belief that his work was sacred (and mindful perhaps of the cheque that would not be in the post), she crept out and gathered them up. Not a word was said when Dylan picked the fragments of paper up from the kitchen table, but later he thanked her. Even Caitlin marvelled at their capacity to make up after an argument and the tender mornings after the raging nights before, but the betrayal with Pearl, a blue-stocking who Caitlin believed had got inside Dylan's mind as well as his body, was a watershed. Their marriage would never be the same again.

*A traditional procession in 1948 around Laugharne
'the strangest town in Wales', according to Thomas,
and the inspiration for his Under Milk Wood*

CHAPTER THIRTEEN
THE TOWN THAT WAS MAD

The strains on Caitlin and Dylan's marriage were not helped by money pressures and lack of work, which was harder for Dylan to find than he had expected. But a BBC producer called Douglas Cleverdon, whom he had worked with before, was encouraging him to work on a project that Dylan had been thinking about for some time – a play for voices about an imaginary town. By October Dylan sent Cleverdon the first forty pages of a work called 'The Town That Was Mad'. It was the only glimmer of hope in what was now a desperate situation. Caitlin decided that they could not cope with another child, and travelled up to London for an abortion in November. Dylan went along with her decision. He was determined to go on a second tour of America with his wife, but while they were happy to leave the older children with friends and relatives, this would not be possible with a small baby. On the day of the procedure, Caitlin drank as much whisky as she could in the pub opposite the private clinic. In a harrowing account of the procedure in *A Warring Absence*, Caitlin claimed that, under a local anaesthetic, the baby was chopped up and removed in chunks. But she was so relieved that she left the clinic the next day feeling 'strong and positively gay'. Dylan was nowhere to be seen.

By the end of the year, only six months after returning from the US, Dylan needed to apply for a grant from the Royal Literary Fund. In letters seeking support from the writer Harold Nicolson and painter Augustus John for the application, Dylan cited the causes being his own ill health (he had been suffering from chest infections), bouncing cheques, two terms' worth of outstanding school fees, a year's rent on his parents' house and the usual unpaid tradesmen's bills. The £300 he was granted (about three quarters of the average annual salary) was immediately swallowed up by these debts.

Some respite was given from both his dire financial and domestic circumstances with a trip to Iran to write film scripts for an oil company. Left alone again, Caitlin started sleeping around with men in Laugharne, partly for sex, and partly, she admitted, for revenge. She confided in Aeron that she was thinking of taking them all to live in Hampshire with the Macnamara clan. Dylan wrote beseechingly to his 'Cattleanchor', begging her not to leave him, grovelling for not providing her with enough money and asking her to be careful not to spend more than £10 a week. Caitlin was having none of it, and when Dylan came back in late February, she found love letters from Pearl in his suitcase. Despite the chaos in his personal life, Dylan managed to write some of his best poems during this time, as well as working on the play for voices about a strange little town. 'Lament' was a rollicking, visceral poem about the transformation of 'a gutsy man and a half' into an 'old ram rod, dying of strangers' via marriage and children. 'Poem on his birthday' refers to 'thirty five bells', so as he was now nearly thirty-seven, he must have been working on it for some time – as the worksheets attest. He would compile long lists of words that rhymed or had similar sounds (assonance), sometimes using a thesaurus, to find the perfect combinations, as well as writing version after version of the work until he was satisfied. The birthday poem is full of beautiful imagery of the Taf estuary, but as Dylan describes the poet 'In his house high on stilts among beaks / And palavers of birds', observing the natural predatory instincts of gulls, herons and fish and the destructive force of nature, he gives a magisterial account of the inevitable progress of life towards death.

In the thistledown fall
He sings towards anguish; finches fly
In the claw tracks of hawks
On a seeing sky; small fishes glide
Through wynds and shells of drowned
Ship towns to pastures of otters.

After he had finished it he went on another work trip to London, and on finding that he could not afford the train fare home, sold the manuscript to a short-lived magazine for £10.

Another poem written this year became one of the most moving and quoted of all English poems. Dylan's father D.J. had recovered from cancer, but as long ago as 1945 Dylan had written a letter to Vernon about his father's ailing health, explaining that he had heart disease, was suffering from unexplained pain, very poor eyesight, and that 'the world that was once the colour of tar to him is now a darker place'. D.J. was in his seventies, and increasingly frail. Dylan saw his parents most days when he was in Laugharne, reading them work in progress at the Pelican, or meeting D.J. at Brown's for a lunchtime pint and the *Times* crossword. Sensing the decline of the father who had nurtured such a deep love of literature in him, he finished another poem, 'Do not go gentle into that good night'.

Do not go gentle into that good night,
Old age should burn and rave at close of day:
Rage, rage against the dying of the light.

It was first published by Marguerite Caetani, Princess of Bassiano, the American-born editor of a Rome-based literary magazine, *Botteghe Oscure*, and the latest wealthy female patron to take an interest in his work. He sent it with a brief note saying that the only person he couldn't show it to was his father, because he didn't know he was dying.

That summer the Boat House received two visitors from America: Brinnin and his lover Bill Read. The plan was to arrange a second tour of America, something Dylan very much wanted. Brinnin was embarrassed to find that Caitlin pressed him for information about Pearl, and when he refused to give any he found her hostility perplexing, as if Dylan's affair was none of her business. Discovering the sleepy little Welsh town of Laugharne and the surrounding countryside was enjoyable, and Brinnin was pleased to hear Dylan read fragments of his play for voices. Dylan was now calling it Llareggub Hill – 'bugger all' spelt backwards, and a nod to his Warmley wordplay with Dan. But witnessing the cycle of physical fights that were forgotten the next day was bewildering. After one particularly violent episode, Caitlin's froideur towards her guests was explained, according to Brinnin, by a long tirade in which she accused him of spoiling her husband and making him big headed. 'They ought to know what he's really like in America, all those fool women, who chase after him while I'm left here to rot in this bloody bog with three screaming children and no money to pay the bills he leaves behind him.' If Dylan was going to make a second trip to America, he would have to take Caitlin with him. By the end of August the date had been fixed for January 1952.

In the meantime, Margaret Taylor had arranged for the family to use the basement flat of a house she had bought in London. It would be easier to keep tabs on the Thomas household closer to home; Dylan would be nearer to his sources of much-needed income, and perhaps less eager to make another tour of America with all its potential risks to his health and marriage. With Dolly the help and her son Desmond in tow, the family arrived at 54 Delancey Street in Camden. Margaret had even managed to

162

arrange for the gypsy caravan from South Leigh to be parked in the garden in the hope that Dylan might do some work. He was sending letters thick and fast seeking financial assistance to settle his debts, yet Caitlin would go out pubbing in the evenings, dressed to the nines in colourful flowing clothes, leaving Aeron to look after Colm once Dolly and Desmond had returned to Laugharne.

It was not a happy experiment. BBC producers were wary of working with Dylan and potential projects fell through. American editors were far more enthusiastic – *Atlantic* magazine was keen to publish his work and paid well – 'Poem in October' earned Dylan $200, while Brinnin had already made more bookings for the next tour. Dylan and Caitlin set sail on the *Queen Mary* on 15 January 1952. Their departure came as a surprise to Aeron, who had no idea why Margaret Taylor came to collect her one day. Her parents had forgotten to tell her that she would be staying with the Taylors in London while they were away. Colm would be going to stay in Laugharne with Dolly.

When John Malcolm Brinnin and a small welcoming party greeted them in New York, bearing a square of red carpet, a box of gardenias for Caitlin and another of cigars for Dylan, they found Dylan dressed in a giant parka, reminding Brinnin of an errant koala bear, and Caitlin decked out in a fur hat and muff like Anna Karenina. The visit got off to a good start, with a ten-day holiday – Brinnin had learned his lesson from the first tour. Much to his relief, Dylan and Caitlin seemed to have put their difficulties behind them. Dylan, the proverbial kid in a sweet shop, enjoyed introducing his wife to pinball, jukeboxes, burgers, hot dogs and umpteen varieties of ice cream. Caitlin had her own project to complete – notes for an 'American Journal' which Dylan had been commissioned to write, and which Brinnin hoped would keep her occupied. But once the inevitable round of dinners and cocktail parties began and Caitlin was exposed to Dylan's adoring ardents, she became withdrawn and hostile, asking Brinnin if Dylan was sleeping with any of them. Resentful that she had had an abortion partly to be able to come with him, she now felt rejected.

Brinnin had to lend them money as they had spent an advance he had sent them before leaving the UK, but this disappeared at an alarming rate. They were staying at the Chelsea Hotel, within striking distance of Greenwich Village and Dylan's American friends. While he went drinking in his favourite unassuming bars, the White Horse Tavern being the most like a Swansea pub, Caitlin would go shopping for clothes and presents for the children in Manhattan's department stores. Clothes had been rationed in the UK up until 1948, and Caitlin enjoyed the chance to splash out so much that they soon accumulated suitcases full. 'I went a bit mad,' she said later. 'I had never seen such abundance.' While Dylan stuck mainly to beer, Caitlin discovered cocktails and rye whiskey, which, combined with the generosity of their hosts and New York's liberal licensing laws, produced disastrous and sometimes bloody results. She admitted that Dylan never pursued women – it was always the other way round – but complained that he never rejected their advances either. His witty, charming banter after readings and at parties may have dazzled the ardents, but it infuriated Caitlin. Perceived rivals were sometimes physically as well as verbally assaulted, and anyone whom Caitlin identified as a 'stuffed shirt', which was a lot of people, was left in no doubt as to her opinion.

The tours left little time for writing, but Dylan talked about finishing his novel, *Adventures in the Skin Trade*, and the renowned English director Michael Powell, who with his partner Emeric Pressburger had made successful films such as *Black Narcissus* and *The Red Shoes*, approached him about an adaptation of a scene from Homer's *Odyssey*. Igor Stravinsky, who was living in Boston and had been introduced to Dylan's work by W.H. Auden, wanted to write the score. The project fell through for lack of funding but Stravinsky was still keen to collaborate with him at some point in the future.

A pitch that did succeed was thanks to some 22-year-old female admirers of Dylan, one of whom worked in publishing. They wanted to make recordings of him reading his work, and with admirable persistence, finally managed to track him down at the Chelsea Hotel at five o'clock one morning just as he was coming back after a night out. At a lunch to discuss the project, Caitlin looked on warily, but the offer of a $500 advance against the first 1,000 records and a 10 per cent royalty thereafter was too good to turn down. Dylan turned up at the studio with only enough material to fill one side of a record. But in her role at *Harper's Bazaar*, Pearl Kazin had bought *A Child's Christmas in Wales* to run as a short story and the magazine's file copy was quickly rustled up for him to read. The Caedmon recordings became classics and helped to make the story one of the most popular ever written in English, and Dylan had inadvertently ensured that the fledgling company would attract recordings by many other significant poets. No one knew at the time how important the recordings would be, not only as marketing tools for Dylan, but also for posterity.

The couple headed off for the west coast via Pennsylvania and Chicago. Dylan had been looking forward to a quieter time in San Francisco with Caitlin on their 'breathless & bloody programme', but it was the scene of one of their worst rows. In a profoundly humiliating episode for Llewelyn, Magdalen College School sent the boy home because his fees had not been paid – although Dylan denied that he had neglected to arrange this. Funds were hastily assembled and the problem was sorted out by the 'lavatory brush', Dylan's nickname for the long-suffering David Higham, on account of his spiky hair, which stood straight up.

Caitlin, aware of how sensitive Llewelyn was, exploded. 'I thought it was outrageous that the prize man in the literary world had had his own son turned out of school for lack of funds when he was being paid huge sums in America, and here we were throwing it around and behaving abominably while Llewelyn was suffering.' She threatened to pack her bags, go home, and leave Dylan forever; overlooking perhaps – or piqued by guilt – that neither of them had ever visited Llewelyn at boarding school, and none of the children heard directly from their mother or father during the four months that they were away. It was a hollow threat. They moved on to Arizona, staying with the surrealist artist Max Ernst, from where they had to cable Brinnin asking for more money. Dylan sent a postcard to Dan in Swansea:

> Caitlin and I are buried in the Tuzigot stone teepee on the other side of this card. We were killed in action, Manhattan Island, Spring 1952, in a valiant battle against American generosity. An American called Double Rye shot Caitlin to death. I was scalped by a Bourbon.

However deadbeat they felt, there were engagements in Vancouver, Chicago and New Orleans before returning to New York. But Brinnin received a call from Dylan saying that he was too exhausted to go to New Orleans, where 800 tickets for his reading had sold out. He agreed to speak personally to make his excuses to the academic who had organised the event – but by the day of the reading he had failed to do so. The word went around academia and the damage to his reputation would cost him – or at least, Brinnin – dear. Yet of the 150 bookings that he eventually made for Dylan in total, this was the only time his performer let him down.

The grand finale at the YM-YWHA Poetry Centre in New York was a resounding success – but a surprise visitor arrived backstage unannounced. It was Dylan's old lover Pearl Kazin, who had left her husband of one year and returned to New York from Mexico, where they had been living. She and Dylan spoke tête-à-tête in the green room, but Brinnin got the impression that whatever Dylan had felt for her before had now passed. Time would show that the same was not true of Pearl. The two men arranged to meet for a farewell drink the night before Dylan was due to leave, but he failed to turn up. As they boarded the ship home, Dylan sent Brinnin a brief thank-you note. Caitlin added that he could keep America. When they arrived back in Laugharne in the early summer of 1952, she had a dazzling new wardrobe and there were stacks of books and huge bags of sweets for the children. But almost all of the thousands of dollars that Dylan had earned over the last four months were gone.

Bout House,
Laugharne,
Carmarthenshire
5 Jan 1953

Dear Fred,

Thank you, very, very much indeed, for writing on my father's death. Poor old boy, he was in awful pain at the end and nearly blind. The day before he died, he wanted to get out of bed & go into the kitchen where his mother was making onion soup for him. Then, a few hours afterwards, he suddenly remembered everything, & where he was, & he said, "It's full circle now."

My mother is very good & brave about it; and she wants to thank you very much, as well, & to wish you a good New Year.

I do hope to see you soon. Ever,
Dylan.

*Thomas's letter to Alfred Janes about the
death of his father, D.J. Thomas*

CHAPTER FOURTEEN
ALL THE RAGE

The year 1952 was one of the most productive of Dylan's life. The Delancey Street episode and the creeping realisation that he was becoming more of a performer of poetry than a writer of it made Laugharne and the solitary confinement of the shed a welcome prospect. He was back in demand at the BBC, and his publisher was pressing for a work in progress that was to provide the introduction to his next volume of poetry. Dylan's excuse was an attack of the lung infection pleurisy, but he finished 'The Prologue', a 102-line tour de force of craftsmanship in praise of the natural world, in which the last line rhymes with the first and the second with the last but one and so on. It used up 166 worksheets. Why Dylan set himself such a difficult task he had no idea, he wrote in a note to his publisher. *Collected Poems* was published in November, just after his thirty-eighth birthday, to great acclaim in the *Sunday Times* and *The Spectator*, with *The Observer* proclaiming him 'the greatest living poet'.

In return for some much needed cash, the Italian magazine *Botteghe Oscure* published a partial version of *Llareggub*, which he was still working on. His script for *The Doctor and the Devils*, the film version of the story of the grave robbers Burke and Hare that he had started work on a decade earlier, was also finished with a view to publication. To cap it all, Dylan was also awarded the coveted Foyle's Literary Prize of £250 for *Collected Poems*. Life seemed calm on the surface, and the summer brought the

169

predictable influx of visitors to the Boat House. There was the biggest audience ever – twenty – for a show put on by the Thomas children and their visiting cousins to entertain the guests, in which Caitlin had a solo dancing spot. Aeron enjoyed rare glimpses of the inside of the hut when she helped her mother 'tidy' the piles of paper on the floor. Letters from famous people were often thrown in the bin – although those Dylan had written were usually kept, and later sold, by their recipients. Caitlin did salvage worksheets, however, as they could already be sold to US collectors.

But the usual undercurrents were swirling below. A large, backdated bill had arrived from the UK tax office, and for Dylan's backlog of unpaid National Insurance contributions. Caitlin was indulging her appetite for casual sex with the locals, and decided to have another abortion in London. It was a much earlier termination than the first one, but it cost, according to Dylan, 'five broadcasts and a loan'. 'The man knocked around inside me with rubber gloves and it was all over very quickly; there was very little to be taken out,' she said matter-of-factly. Dylan tripped on the Boat House steps and broke his arm. But a much harder blow fell at the end of the year, when D.J. died.

It came as no surprise as the old man, now seventy-six, had been ailing fast since Dylan's return from the US. But Dylan was devastated. D.J. was an atheist who requested that he be cremated and have his ashes buried next to his brother in the little mining town of Pontypridd in the Rhondda valley. Dylan found the ceremony deeply disturbing, especially when he was apparently told afterwards that his father's head had exploded in the furnace. There were letters of condolence from Vernon and Fred, to which Dylan wrote fond replies. He told Vernon how much he missed his father and let him know of his plans to read three of his friend's poems in a broadcast from Swansea in the new year, when he hoped to see him. Fred learned of how, in his confusion, D.J. had gone into the kitchen of the Pelican just before he died, thinking his mother was making him onion soup. Later in bed he came to and said: 'It's full circle now'.

Brown's Hotel was not the same without D.J. and Dylan doing the crossword over their morning pint, and Ivy the landlady mentioned to Caitlin how depressed Dylan seemed. He still went to Pelican House in the morning to keep Florence company, and it was here that he wrote much of *Under Milk Wood*. 'I can remember him talking to me, very quiet and subdued,' Caitlin wrote, 'saying that all he had ever learnt he had learnt from his father, and saying it with greater respect and affection than I had ever seen before'.

A few months earlier, John Malcolm Brinnin had been passing through London. He and Dylan had met, and despite all Brinnin's misgivings, Dylan persuaded him that another tour of America was a good idea to promote the publication of *Collected Poems* in March. They hatched a plot for readings of his play for voices as a novelty for the US, but as they chatted on the top of a bus on the way to Waterloo station, where Brinnin was to catch the boat train for France, the American suggested that the jokey title *Llareggub* would be lost on US audiences. 'What about *Under Milk Wood*?' Dylan replied. It took Dylan six months to follow up the conversation, writing with a litany of excuses that included Caitlin's abortion, his father's death, publishers demanding overdue work and Margaret Taylor wanting to sell the Boat House, which had caused a tearful row. Caitlin was dead against the trip, accusing Dylan of going to the US only for 'flattery, idleness and infidelity'. He was stung and replied that the right words were 'appreciation, dramatic work and friends'. The only thing that would placate her was the offer of a long holiday in Portugal afterwards without the children. Dylan wrote to Brinnin in March

171

1953 to say that as long as this was possible, and the tour could last only six weeks, he didn't mind how much he read, or how often or where.

Aeron heard Dylan practising his readings in the bathroom of the Boat House. There was talk of everyone moving to California, where Dylan would work with Stravinsky or take up a possible post at a university there. His departure was set for April 1953, but before leaving he had an important date at the BBC in Cardiff – the recording of his first ever TV programme called '*Home Town – Swansea*'. It was based on the earlier on the earlier group broadcast he had made for BBC radio at The Grove studios. Several of Dylan's recent broadcasts had been made there, and he and Caitlin sometimes stayed with Dan and Irene, who now lived in Rosehill Terrace, perched high above the town but not far from the studios. Dan had by now composed the third of his cycle of twelve symphonies, each centred on a semitone of the chromatic scale. His brilliance had already been rewarded with a prize from the Royal Philharmonic Society for his 'Symphonic Prologue', commissions for the Festival of Britain and other prestigious events. But there was still time to relive the old Warmley days. He and Dylan revisited the Uplands 'itch pit', played cricket with Dylan junior in the back garden, breaking a window in the process, or messed around with Dan's wire recorder, a machine that could record audio using fine steel wire. One of the fragile old wires has been converted to a CD by Dan's daughter Cathrin and on it Dylan can be heard reading 'Do not go gentle into that good night' and 'In the White Giant's Thigh'. Mellowed by evenings at the pub, they also recorded impromptu plays in which Caitlin and Irene would take part too, putting on silly voices to a background of suppressed giggles.

The Cardiff film centred around Fred's portraits of Vernon, Dan and Dylan. Wynford Vaughan Thomas, an older Swansea

Grammar School boy and Little Theatre chum who had read history at Oxford and become a senior BBC reporter, was the link man, but the programme was largely unscripted. Dylan wrote careful notes about the set-up and directions about who would speak with the practised eye of a professional filmmaker. The set was a mock-up of Fred's studio, with the painter at his easel, Vernon on a chair, Dan at a piano and Dylan on a sofa. Each spoke in turn about what they had been thinking about while Fred had painted them. Dan's and Vernon's portraits were fairly recent, but Dylan's set him off on a long reminiscence. The BBC did not archive all its programmes, so no copy of the film exists – or indeed any of Dylan – but his part was reproduced in an article by Vernon for the *Texas Quarterly* journal of the University of Texas at Austin.

It was a terrible long time ago. Before television … Before radio even, I shouldn't be surprised when I see that dewy goblin portrait frog-goggling at me out of the past. (I think that portrait must have been losing weight: I can hardly recognise it now.) Before the internal combustion engine, before the invention of the wheel, oh what a long nice time ago in the Golden Days. Do you remember them Fred? The Golden Days in London, when we were exiled Bohemian boily boys. There were three of us then, you and me and Mervyn Levy, three very young monsters green and brimming from Swansea, stiff with lyrics and ambitions and still lifes, all living together in one big bare barmy beautiful room kept by a Mrs Parsnip, as far as I can remember, in Redcliffe Gardens. Two of us had beards, and I grew one too, sparse and ginger and limp, like a depressed marmalade cat with the mange; I don't know what happened to it; either it fell off, or was blown off, or it just grew in, I can't remember. Mervyn had a different beard every fortnight, and everyone his own: spade-shaped, Assyrian, Captain Kettle,

Victorian-celebrity, rabbi, Uncle Sam goatee, Southern Gentleman, goat; and once he had only a half beard, oiled and curled and scented, on one side of his face; but nobody seemed to notice in that neighbourhood, which was infuriating. Mrs Parsnip was always boiling cabbage downstairs, cabbage and lights [lungs], and maybe, mice; and one of us was painting mackerel mackerel all the time, day in day out, the same mackerel too, until they used to get up and walk around the room, just like real live models ... Mervyn Levy was an art student, and just beginning other experiments; Janes was practising mackerel and jujitsu; and I was writing poems (of a kind) for immortality and the Poets' Corner of the *Sunday Referee*. What we cooked I don't know, unless it was our next-door neighbours, miaows and all, but it tasted like the Ritz. There was no weather in those Golden Days, only light and dark, loud and soft, miserable and bouncing. We hadn't got any money at all, and, to show you how young we were, even that was delightful: or is this middle age talking, looking back through a ring-o'-roses?

Well anyway, there we were. That's when that portrait of me, a frog in his salad days, was painted. And those were the days that we, now, we get so nostalgic about. But in those London days, I remember, we were terribly nostalgic, too, about our town, Swansea, that we had left for ever and ever. And here we are, back again.

A few days later, Dylan was off again, setting sail for New York on 16 April, leaving David Higham in charge of paying the bills at home. The manuscript of *Under Milk Wood* – which he had left in a briefcase after a reading in Cardiff, to be retrieved by a friend after frantic messages – was to be finished on the boat in time for its first full reading with actors in New York. The start of Dylan's third visit to America in three years followed a now-familiar pattern; checking into a room at the Chelsea Hotel, followed by a tour of his favourite bars, ending up at the White Horse. Later at the fashionable Algonquin Hotel, his presence caused a buzz, and although he dismissed his celebrity status as a joke, he was clearly pleased. Brinnin had lost his appetite for chaperoning Dylan around another tightly packed schedule and left him pretty much to his own devices, but there was a new face on the scene: a clever, worldly arts graduate who had worked in the theatre and who was now Brinnin's new assistant at the YH-YWHA Poetry Centre.

Liz Reitell was charged with making sure that the premier solo reading of *Under Milk Wood* took place in New York as scheduled. When she first met the 'tousled little drunk' she took an instant dislike to him, and he seemed rather frightened of her, but her business-like approach worked. She regularly telephoned Brinnin's empty apartment in Boston, where Dylan stayed on the first leg of his tour, to check on his progress, and Dylan got on with the job. The pressure was enormous. He had not only to finish the work, but then faced reading, solo, the part of the narrator as well as the multitude of characters, male and female, solemn and comic as the play takes the listener through a day in the life of an eccentric little seaside town. It would call on all of Dylan's considerable talents as an actor and mimic.

His first poetry readings were to take place around Boston, including one at Harvard's revered Fogg Museum. Dylan was anxious beforehand but the reading, according to Brinnin, was one of his best ever, with rapturous applause between poems in the rammed auditorium. Dylan's first solo reading of *Under Milk Wood* – still unfinished – was greeted with similar delight there on 3 May, in an atmosphere of 'crackling excitement' interrupted by gales of laughter, according to Brinnin.

The value put on his work was demonstrated by a publisher who had been printing extracts of his unfinished novel, *Adventures in the Skin Trade,* in the US, and was prepared to pay up to $4,000 for the finished work. From the advance Dylan immediately sent $250 to Caitlin in addition to another $100 that he had sent almost as soon as he had arrived. In the accompanying letter he complained that he had done fourteen readings in as many days on a hectic run up and down the east coast. It was full of the adoring, pleading declarations that she was all too used to receiving while he was away. Her response was stony silence – and her instincts were right: Pearl Kazin was back in town. She and Dylan had met briefly in New York and now, to Brinnin's surprise, she turned up in Boston to spend a day and a night with Dylan, causing much gossip among the partygoers they mixed with after a reading at the Massachusetts Institute of Technology.

There was a hectic overnight trip to South Carolina for another reading, followed by an appearance in Connecticut before Dylan was due in New York to meet Reitell and the cast she was already rehearsing. Despite her exhortations Dylan had still failed to complete the script, unsurprisingly given his back-to-back commitments since arriving. Now he got up early in the morning to work on it, writing whole new scenes on scraps of paper in his room and on the train on the way to New York. On the day of the performance, there was an afternoon rehearsal, followed by an early evening run-through. Dylan was still writing scenes at five o'clock in the afternoon with two typists organised by Liz on hand to make them legible. It was too much for Dylan, who by then felt too shattered to go on, but when Liz threatened to cancel the premiere, Dylan baulked and in a desperate final push wrote final scenes that were still being typed up and handed to the cast after the play had begun.

At first the 1,000-strong audience was uncertain. The opening description by First Voice (the narrator) of the small town asleep is slow and incantatory. Would this be the tone of the whole evening?

> To begin at the beginning:
>   It is spring, moonless night in the small town, starless and bible-black, the cobblestreets silent and the hunched, courters'-and-rabbits' wood limping invisible down to the sloeblack, slow, black, crowblack, fishingboat-bobbing sea.

The first character to speak is Captain Cat, a blind, retired sea captain who is visited in his sleep by his drowned sailor friends. But as they were introduced to the other forty-odd inhabitants of Cockle Row and Donkey Street such as Mr Mog Edwards, 'a draper mad with love', frustrated schoolteacher Gossamer Beyon and their often erotic dreamworlds, the audience began to realise that it was also funny, surreal and affectionate. They started laughing and continued laughing until the end. Brinnin wrote:

> When the lights slowly faded and the night had swallowed up the last face and muffled the last voice in the village, there was an unexpected silence both on stage and off. The thousand spectators sat as if stunned, as if the slightest handclap might violate a spell. But within a few moments the lights went up and applause crescendoed and bravos were shouted by half the standing audience while the cast came back for curtain call after curtain call until, at the fifteenth of these, squat and boyish in his happily flustered modesty, Dylan stepped out alone.

The author's account in a letter to Caitlin a week later played down his triumph: 'I've finished that infernally eternally unfinished "Play" and have done it in New York with actors.'

DYLAN THOMAS

Collected Poems

1934–1952

LONDON
J. M. DENT & SONS LTD

When the artist Ceri Richards heard that Thomas was seriously ill in
New York in 1953, he made drawings in his copy of Collected Poems,
like this one of the poet looking out from the Boat House in Laugharne

CHAPTER FIFTEEN

TROUBLE AND STRIFE

Brinnin's account of the next few days paints a picture of Dylan happier and more relaxed than he had ever seen him – and hardly drinking anything. Buoyed up by the reception of *Under Milk Wood*, he was also very excited by the revival of the plan to work with Stravinsky. The composer had been conducting a performance of *The Rite of Spring* in Boston and had invited Dylan to discuss it. Redolent of the anxiety generated by the Cold War, their idea was to tell the story of two humans recreating the world completely anew from the ruins of global warfare or some kind of nuclear event. Dylan was sketching it all out in his mind: Boston University would commission it and the money, $1,000 for the completed work, plus a first-class passage and royalties, would enable Dylan to work with the composer on it at his Hollywood home, while Caitlin stayed with friends in San Francisco.

The euphoria was short lived. Once back in New York for the final reading of *Under Milk Wood*, he fell down some stairs, broke an arm again and was struck by another of his recurring attacks of gout. Liz Reitell was trying to make sure that he stayed out of trouble, and he was clearly grateful for her ministrations, but it was obvious that she was now far more than his producer-cum-minder-cum-nurse. Dylan wore his arm in a black sling for the last performance of a more complete version of *Under Milk Wood*, but the strain of the last few weeks showed when he turned chalk white afterwards and was violently sick thanks to another of his chronic health problems: alcoholic gastritis, an inflammation of the lining of the stomach. Dr Milton Feltenstein, Liz Reitell's physician, was called to give him pain-relieving shots for his broken arm and gout. He urged Dylan to get help in London to lead what we would now call a healthy lifestyle.

Dylan's homecoming in June was a repeat of the last one: Caitlin wanted to celebrate; Dylan, tired out, just wanted to go home. Aeron, who often stayed with Florence now, snuggling up in her grandmother's bed, noticed that even after a few weeks away her father's health had deteriorated. The cough that racked him in the mornings was far worse and left him wheezing like a pair of bellows, and there were reports from Brown's that he had been suffering from blackouts.

In July she accompanied her parents on a trip to the National Eisteddfod in north Wales, which Dylan was covering for the BBC. Aeron was impressed by the druids in their flowing white robes but even more so by a pretty young woman in a floral dress and high heels who approached them in the huge marquee. It was the Queen, who smiled sweetly at the little girl, chatted politely and sent her mother's warm regards to Dylan. Later in the summer, she went to Brown's to watch Dylan's first solo TV performance on the hotel's little nine-inch black-and-white set, when he read 'The Outing' (also known as 'A Story'), the tale of an uncle who was 'big and trumpeting and red-hairy and used to fill every inch of the hot little house like an old buffalo squeezed into an airing cupboard'. The old man plans an outing with his cronies to the seaside resort of Porthcawl, but they never get there, the pubs on the way proving too much of a distraction. Caitlin later had an affair with the young cameraman.

Dylan soon wrote to Reitell telling her how much he missed her (though with none of the passion with which he wrote to his wife), and carefully asked her to send personal, rather than business, letters to the Savage Club. Caitlin, meanwhile, was trying to get back in control of her life by sending Aeron to an expensive performing arts boarding school in England where she could vicariously resurrect her mother's broken dream of becoming a dancer. Caitlin planned to return to Elba with Colm to renew her friendship with the innkeeper of the *pensione* from their Italian trip six years earlier.

Word of *Under Milk Wood*'s success in New York had spread and publishers were clamouring for the rights. The script of *The Doctor and the Devils* had been published while Dylan was away and was selling well. A US agent was offering $1,000 a week for a lecture tour, but until the funds for the project with Stravinsky were forthcoming, the future was still uncertain. A decision was made when Brinnin arrived in Laugharne in September to write a profile of Dylan for an American magazine that was paying $750 for extracts from *Under Milk Wood*. He brought Rollie McKenna with him, a photographer who had shot Dylan in New York. Dylan obliged by taking them on a tour with Florence around the countryside of his childhood. They visited the new owner of Fernhill, picking windfall apples in the orchard laden with fruit, and called on an extended family of cousins, whose kitchen was hung with flitches of bacon and housed a fireplace big enough for five men to stand in.

After drinking cups of warm milk fresh from the cow, they were ushered into a room lined with shelves of china, to meet a tiny old woman dressed in black silk. Florence spoke to her deferentially in Welsh – she knew no English – and the two Americans, despite understanding nothing, were struck by the matriarchal dignity of the elderly lady, who, they were told, was ninety-six. Further along the country lanes they stopped at the gate of Florence's old family home, Blaencwm, to greet an old man, a brother of Florence's who lived alone. She promised to make her yearly visit to help him tidy up the house. Before getting back to Laugharne they visited a graveyard where they could hear the murmurs of the evening service taking place in the chapel. Florence walked among the headstones on her two sticks, pointing out the names of family members to Dylan, betraying little of the emotion she must have felt. She had lost not only her husband within the last year, but her daughter Nancy, who had gone to live in India, where she and her officer husband had met during the war. Nancy had died of cancer on the same day in April that Dylan had left for New York.

McKenna's photographs tell an idyllic tale of a poet and his family at home in the land of *Under Milk Wood*. The magazine's readers in America would surely want to hear it performed so another tour was mooted, only three months after Dylan had returned in such poor shape from the last one. Brinnin claimed that he only agreed with the greatest reluctance, and under pressure from Dylan. Caitlin was dead against it. As far as she was concerned, another US visit was on the condition that they would live in California so Dylan could work with Stravinsky, but now he had reneged on the deal. Aeron witnessed her mother calling Dylan a bloody bastard and punching him in the head. Vernon, too, saw a shocking eruption when he visited Dylan that summer. He asked Dylan to read 'Over Sir John's Hill', the first poem that he had written on returning to Laugharne after the war. As Dylan read softly, Caitlin interrupted to pick him up on the pronunciation of a word, and as their bickering escalated into a screaming match, little Colm burst into tears and Aeron fled the room. By the time Dylan set off in October, Aeron had left for boarding school, where he wrote to her saying how much he missed her and Llewelyn, and asking what she would like him to bring back from America. He stopped off in Swansea on the way to London and called in on 'Ralph the Books' shop to order their Christmas annuals.

A few days before his departure on 19 October, Fred and Mary arrived with an old friend who had been wanting to meet Dylan for some time. The artist Ceri Richards admired the poet enormously and had produced a series of lithographs inspired by his 1933 poem 'The force that through the green fuse drives the flower', for the 1947 issue of the influential *Poetry London* magazine. Vernon knew Ceri well too and had talked to him a lot about Dylan, and wanted to introduce them, but somehow they had never met.

Like Dylan and his grammar school friends, Ceri came from Swansea, where his father was a tin-plate worker and conducted both the male voice and chapel choirs in the village of Dunvant, where the family lived. Ceri, who was a decade older than Dylan, had shown, like Fred, a natural gift for drawing and painting as a child, and had later studied at Swansea School of Art under its ambitious and visionary principal, Grant Murray.

At a summer school at Gregynog Hall in mid-Wales, where two remarkable Welsh sisters had turned their home into a centre for the arts, the wonderful collection of Impressionist painters the heiresses had collected had come as a revelation to young Ceri. He went on to study in the design school at the Royal College of Art and his graphic skills, rich sense of colour and powerful, flowing line coalesced in the illustrations for *Poetry London*, in which he incorporated the words of the poem in his flowing hand. By the summer of 1953 Ceri had taken up a teaching post at Chelsea School of Art alongside Henry Moore and Graham Sutherland. In an exhibition at the prestigious Redfern contemporary art gallery in Mayfair in 1946, he had shown paintings that were named after 'The force that through the green fuse drives the flower'. In the holidays he returned to Gower with his young family to stay in their holiday bungalow in Pennard, not far from the Watkins tribe. He and Vernon shared the deep love of the Gower landscape that inspired so much of their work, as well as of Dylan's poetry, and soon became close friends.

183

When Fred discovered that Ceri had never met Dylan, he offered to drive him down to Laugharne. Ceri was in any case eager to discuss a proposal to put on a show of his illustrations of Dylan's poetry, accompanied by readings, at the Glynn Vivian Art Gallery in Swansea. Fred and Mary were looking forward to another of the immensely enjoyable trips they made to see Dylan, when Ross would play with Llewelyn on the beach, and they were always taken to the Pelican to see Florence and D.J. when he was still alive. But the atmosphere this time was chilly. 'When we arrived at the Boat House, we sat out on the verandah and Mary asked Caitlin if she was looking forward to going to America. "I am NOT going to America," she replied in a voice that silenced us all,' Fred recalled. A little later Dolly the help brought a lunch of stew and potatoes. Caitlin had disappeared. She had taken a book and was sitting on the sand below the Boat House, reading. 'Later Dylan wanted to go for a drive. We went down to Amroth [a village further west along the coast], visiting a few pubs on the way. We came back to Brown's Hotel and as we were leaving, the last thing Dylan said to me was "I'm only going to pay the bills".

It was the only time that Ceri would meet Dylan. He wrote to Vernon afterwards to tell him how much he had enjoyed his visit to the beautiful but melancholy Boat House, which Dylan filled with his 'resounding voice and friendliness,' adding: 'I think we would have come to like one another very much and I would love to have had other meetings with him … but if I had missed him then I would have been filled with regret'. Ceri went on to have a stellar career, selling internationally and exhibiting at one-man shows in national galleries such as the Whitechapel and the Tate in London, which owns several important examples of his work. Despite their brief meeting, Dylan remained a lifelong major source of inspiration for Ceri. Of all the countless tributes and references to his poetry by other creative artists in all fields, Ceri's are some of the finest.

One of the drawings Ceri Richards made in his copy of Dylan's
Collected Poems

Dylan did, indeed, have bills to pay, and letters were sent to friends, including Dan, as well as publishers asking for loans or advances. At least *Under Milk Wood* was finished in time for the tour, but it was the cause of a final spat between Dylan and Caitlin. Dylan had managed to lose the handwritten manuscript in London a few days earlier. Thankfully, the BBC producer Douglas Cleverdon had already arranged for a secretary to duplicate it before Dylan left, and turned up at the airline bus terminal with three copies just as Caitlin was berating her husband. Dylan was so relieved that he told Cleverdon to keep the manuscript if he ever found it, and suggested where he might look. It didn't take long for the producer to claim his reward in a Soho pub. Years later, Dylan's grateful gesture produced bitter consequences.

On 5 November Caitlin was sitting in the village hall, where a local audience had gathered to hear a BBC broadcast called, simply, 'Laugharne' that Dylan had written before he left. Affectionate and entertaining as ever, it expressed his feelings for the town that had been his home, on and off, for more than five years. As Caitlin listened someone slipped her a telegram. It stated simply that Dylan had been hospitalised. It was a word that she didn't recognise at first, so she put the telegram in her pocket to deal with later and spent the evening partying.

Dylan had arrived in New York on 20 October and walked straight into the arms of Brinnin's assistant, Liz Reitell. They pottered quietly around the city for a couple of days, rehearsing for the performance of *Under Milk Wood* that was to take place at the Poetry Centre on 24 October. Dylan was drinking far less than usual. What happened over the next two weeks has been the source of immense speculation ever since, with claims, counter-claims, accusations and their rebuttal filling entire books. What is clear is that Dylan felt increasingly unwell, shivering under blankets during one rehearsal, at which Reitell had to take his place. His bad chest wasn't helped by the autumnal smog that was enveloping New York. Her response was to give him the sedative phenobarbitone to help him sleep, and when he had still not improved on the day of the opening performance of the play, she arranged for her physician, Dr Feltenstein, to administer what Dylan described as his 'winking needle'. The injections included ACTH, a hormone that triggers the production of natural steroids, to help relieve Dylan's painful gout, and amphetamine to boost his energy. He perked up enough to go to the next rehearsal, but Brinnin, who was keeping his distance and had entrusted Dylan's care to Reitell, was alarmed by Dylan's pallor and sunken eyes. The agent was disappointed by the first reading, but a matinée the next day in front of a thousand people, was, he thought, the best yet.

By now the usual hectic round of live performances and appearances was in train, sandwiched between parties and dinners.

A predictable cycle of behaviour kicked in – Dylan could be at a low ebb one minute, then rally the next; outrageous after a few drinks or utterly charming. At a symposium on poetry and film in the company of intellectuals including Arthur Miller he was in fine form, and had the audience in fits with his self-deprecating responses to the often pretentious comments of the other panellists. But he felt so poorly on the evening of his thirty-ninth birthday on 27 October that he spent it berating himself in his hotel bedroom for leaving an elaborate dinner party that friends were holding for him.

After cocktails one evening to discuss possible commercial theatre productions of *Under Milk Wood* and *Adventures in the Skin Trade*, he was exhausted and went to bed. He slept fitfully until 2 a.m. when he told Reitell he needed a drink and would be back in half an hour. Two hours later he came back saying that he had drunk eighteen straight whiskeys – a boast that soon became legendary, but is in all likelihood untrue. The poet, whom his ex-girlfriend Pamela Hansford Johnson had witnessed pretending to be drunk all those years ago in Chelsea, was exaggerating. According to the bartender at the White Horse, who served Dylan from a bottle of Old Grand-Dad whiskey, he had drunk no more than six measures (25ml if these were standard 1 fluid ounce measures). That would equate to about six units of alcohol by today's standards, the equivalent of about two thirds of a bottle of wine.

The next day, 4 November, Dylan felt too ill to keep a lunch date, but went with Reitell to the White Horse for a couple of beers, where he felt sick and had to go back to the hotel. Dr Feltenstein was called three times to see Dylan, who kept vomiting and complained that he was suffocating. The doctor's winking needle administered more ACTH and when Dylan began to hallucinate, half a grain (about 30mg) of morphine sulphate to relieve pain and put him to sleep. That was an unusually high dose for anyone not used to taking it. Morphine is in any case not a drug that should be prescribed to heavy drinkers or people with breathing difficulties as it can also depress the respiratory system and thus starve the brain of oxygen. Reitell stayed with Dylan through the evening. At around midnight he started to have difficulty breathing and his face turned blue. Instead of calling an ambulance, she called Feltenstein, but he was not available. The police were called, who in turn called an ambulance, but the delay meant that it was two hours before it deposited Dylan, now in a coma, at St Vincent's Hospital.

Brinnin was horror-struck to receive a call in Boston in the early hours of the morning from Reitell, who was hysterical. It is not hard to imagine the panic that she must have felt. She may have accomplished her task of ensuring that the thousands of people who had bought tickets for *Under Milk Wood* were not disappointed, but now its stellar creator, with whom she was also having an illicit affair, had fallen unconscious on her watch. Brinnin got straight on the next plane, and it was his account of what happened next that helped set the 'eighteen straight whiskeys' story in stone. At first, he said, the doctors suspected a cerebral haemorrhage, then a 'diabetic shock', but blood sugar tests soon ruled that out. Next it was 'a severe insult to the brain' caused by suspected alcohol poisoning – although it could have been the result of oxygen deprivation exacerbated by the morphine. Feltenstein arrived, despite having no authority in the hospital, and thought, worryingly, that the coma indicated the severity of the brain damage, but the young hospital doctors in charge, on the other hand, suggested that the longer Dylan remained alive, the greater his chances of recovery.

Confusion reigned, but what no one seemed to have noticed was that Dylan's notes recorded X-rays taken on admission that showed

188

he was already suffering from bronchial pneumonia. This alone could have explained his earlier feverishness – the shivering fits alternating with a temperature that reached 105.5°F (40.8°C) – and coughing spasms so severe that they tore blood vessels and produced bloody vomit. Leaving this untreated was taking a very serious risk indeed. Without access to Dylan's medical history, the doctors were in ignorance of his recurrent chest infections, and had to rely instead on what Reitell and Feltenstein told (and didn't tell) them – which, according to the notes, emphasised how much Dylan drank. All this was not pieced together until painstaking research fifty years later by the writer David N. Thomas.

Word that Dylan Thomas was critically ill soon got out and crossed the Atlantic, but at such a remove it was hard to keep pace with events. Dylan had stayed in Swansea with Dan Jones before he left. He recalled that while he seemed well enough, he had a bad gash on his forehead, the result of an incident in a London nightclub when Dylan had, Dan believed, been hit on the head with a table-lamp. He cabled a brain specialist who had been called in to help with the diagnosis at St Vincent's, to suggest that perhaps Dylan was suffering from concussion and brain damage. Later they spoke on the phone via intermediaries who were more used to making transatlantic phone calls than Dan, who was in any case facing a recital of a very challenging piece of music in a few days' time. When the subject of Dylan's drinking came up the specialist confirmed that this was now the sole focus of his treatment. Dan's own doctor spoke to the specialist and while he told Dan that a tracheotomy had been performed to assist's Dylan's breathing, he spared him the information that the coma would have inflicted severe brain damage.

Ceri Richards heard the news and wrote to Vernon of his concern: 'It appears to be very critical – we only hope that by some miracle he will survive and come back to Wales very soon.' As Ceri waited he took several copies of the *Collected Poems* and made pen and ink drawings that framed the lines on their pages. Dylan's critical condition had made the artist all the more aware of the poet's preoccupation with death. 'I have tried to meet imagery with imagery and meaning with meaning,' he told Vernon.

By now Caitlin had been telephoned and was in London on her way to New York, with the cost of her air fare guaranteed by Dan and Vernon. The ever-vigilant Margaret Taylor pulled strings to make sure that she got a visa and flight as quickly as possible. But whether she would get there before Dylan died was in doubt. Brinnin used his contacts to try and ensure that she got through immigration as fast as possible. When she arrived at St Vincent's, a Catholic institution, she was, in her own words, 'stinking drunk'. Brinnin got there at about the same time. 'Is the bloody man dead yet?' she asked him. She still had no idea of the existence of Liz Reitell, who kept out of her way.

A crowd had gathered at the hospital to wait for news, craning through a glass pane in the door to see Dylan in his oxygen tent. As Caitlin walked past them she recognised hardly anyone. Once she entered the room and heard her husband fighting for breath, the finality of the situation hit her. His face was covered with tubes and an oxygen mask. All she could really see was his hands, 'those two little fishes fins stuck out from the cover of his bed'. She tried to roll a cigarette but her own hands were shaking too much. She pressed her body to his so that he could feel her warmth but a nurse quickly pulled her off, saying it would suffocate him. After about fifteen minutes she left the room and started banging her head against a window in the corridor which was reinforced with wire mesh and, thankfully, didn't smash. She was led to an adjoining room where according to Brinnin, someone plied her with whisky. Fuelled by the alcohol, Caitlin assaulted him, tore a crucifix from the wall and smashed a statue of the Virgin Mary. After biting the hand of an orderly and attacking the doctor who had been summoned to deal with her, she was put in a straitjacket. Feltenstein was summoned and decided that Caitlin was a danger to herself and others, and arranged to have her committed to a psychiatric clinic. Liz Reitell resumed her vigil at Dylan's bedside.

Dylan died peacefully at 1 p.m. the next day. The only person there was the poet John Berryman, an old friend. He wrote to Vernon to explain what had happened. 'His body was utterly quiet, and he looked so tired that you once more might have burst into tears too, but your grief would have been general, for the whole catastrophe, not for the moment.'

PART THREE

DID NOT GO GENTLE

Dylan Thomas by Alfred Janes, 1964

CHAPTER SIXTEEN

SIX FEET DEEP

The large table in a front room of a handsome Edwardian house in Dulwich Village is covered in pots and tubes of paint, rags, old jam jars full of brushes, screws and nails. There are more jars on the mantelpiece above a pretty fireplace that has been covered over with a two-bar electric fire. Mary loathes what she perceives as a mess and calls the room that Fred has commandeered as a studio 'the tramp's nest'. He is perched on a stool in front of his easel, working from memory and a few black-and-white photos on his third and final portrait of Dylan – a pen-and-ink drawing that will appear in the *Spectator* magazine to illustrate an article by the author of the first full-length biography of the poet, Constantine Fitzgibbon.

Fred had left Wales for south London the year before – 1963. The old Gower farmhouse that he had moved to ten years earlier, and where he had painted his second portrait of Dylan, was an idyllic place to live with its beautiful views across fields and woods to the curve of Oxwich Bay. But the plan to run part of it as a guesthouse in a joint venture with family members had faltered, and Fred and Mary found themselves responsible for a large property with four acres of land but unable to afford much hired help or buy labour-saving devices like dishwashers or tumble driers, which were still rudimentary, or had not yet been invented. The drudgery for Mary of 1950s housework in a damp old farmhouse was hard enough without having extra rooms to clean and more wet sheets to wring through a hand-turned mangle. When the offer of a part-time teaching job for Fred in London came up, it was now or never.

Dan had gone to meet Dylan's body when it arrived back at Southampton on the SS United States. Caitlin had regained enough sanity to be discharged from the psychiatric clinic and was determined to bring her husband's body back to Wales. After being consigned to the ship's hold after some outlandish drinking and dancing on the upper decks, she had slept in a bunk next to Dylan's coffin. It was in a crate that the unsuspecting sailors used as a card table. Ebie Williams, the landlord of Brown's Hotel, drove Dan to Southampton. It was dark when they reached the dock, but he could make out crew members with balloons and streamers – the remnants of the last-night party on board. Further down the side of the boat, other crew members lowered the crate on to the quay alongside the waiting hearse. If Dan and Caitlin travelled back to Laugharne together, he didn't mention it. In fact he did not mention her name once in his 1976 memoir about his friend. For now he did his best to support Caitlin, but by the time he wrote *My Friend Dylan Thomas*, their relationship had changed radically.

Dylan's body was taken to the Pelican, where his mother Florence calmly showed guests to the front room to pay their respects. She seemed content to explain that Dylan's health had never been good, and no one had the heart to tell her what had really happened. The rumours that he had died of alcohol poisoning were rife, but few had seen the post mortem report, which revealed how poor Dylan's physical state was in general and concluded that the causes of death were swelling of the brain, a fatty liver and broncho pneumonia. In a way Florence was right – these were symptoms of chronic poor health that had been developing for some time, but like everyone else at the time she was ignorant of the damage that Dylan's smoking, drinking, sugar-laden diet and lack of exercise were inflicting. The medical research highlighting these risk factors did not exist, or was in its infancy.

American morticians had done their best to keep up appearances. They had dressed Dylan in an executive suit and bow tie, and covered his face with thick make-up, rouge and lipstick. He was wearing a fresh red carnation – the result of a bet with Ebie Williams that whichever man died first would place one in the buttonhole of the other. The funeral took place on 25 November at St Martin's Church, where Dylan's children, Llewelyn, Aeron and Colm, had all been christened. None of the children were there. Colm was too young, at still only four. Fourteen-year-old Llewelyn was told of his father's death by his headmaster at Magdalen College School, and not invited to the funeral – a cause of bitter resentment. Caitlin dispatched her sister, Nicolette Devas, to visit Aeron at the Arts Educational School in Hertfordshire, where she was boarding. It took her aunt a little while to get to the point and when ten-year-old Aeron finally understood what had happened, said nothing but concentrated on stopping herself being sick.

A Pathé newsreel of the funeral shows a long procession of mourners walking four-deep behind the coffin bearers up the path to the church. Caitlin clings to Dan, who in his admittedly self-appointed role of funeral tsar, holds her tightly at the graveside, while Fred stands just behind them. Friends from the Kardomah days joined Florence for tea and homemade cake at the Pelican afterwards, where, with remarkable composure, she read out the letters, cards and telegrams of condolence she had received – after the loss of her husband D.J. and daughter Nancy, this was her third bereavement in less than a year. The mourners later gathered at Brown's, where, in the mêlée, Caitlin knocked a tray of pints all over Fred. Charlie Fisher was there. 'His wake would have made a fine story,' he observed, 'if Dylan could have written it'. Florence discovered afterwards that Dylan's own edition of his *Collected Poems* and another limited edition of poems that he had inscribed to his parents had been stolen from the house. Some time later a university lecturer from Swansea came with an empty attaché case to buy up books and manuscripts which he coveted, but Florence sent him away. He was later found at the Boat House by her son-in-law, going through papers while Caitlin went for a swim.

The Times had telephoned Vernon Watkins just before Dylan died to ask him to write an obituary. Unlike other reports which focused on sensational biographical details, he chronicled his output in poetry, film and on the radio. It was, wrote his wife Gwen, the greatest loss of Vernon's life. Much later he wrote: 'The true tragedy of Dylan's death is that he died. Everything else is secondary to that.' In a short tribute Fred wrote:

> To him a personality was a world – a wide world, in which some stay at home and others walk abroad. He, in his span took it upon himself to climb every mountain, to go down every pit and to turn up every stone; he was at home in the jungles and familiar with the poles and when he died it was not the first time he had reached his own world's end.
>
> What he learned was hammered into his work and it is there that one had best look for his true merit. It takes great courage and honesty and faith to tell what one has found, not only in the bright places, but also in the holes and corners of one's soul.

In other accounts the *New York Times* described Dylan as 'the best of the younger poets who wrote in English, meaning the generation after T.S. Eliot and W.H. Auden'. Newspapers like the *Daily Express* and *Manchester Guardian* pointed out the exceptional commercial success of his poetry – in 1953 and before his death in November, *Collected Poems* had sold 10,000 copies, whereas 300 would have kept most publishers happy. Even Philip Larkin acknowledged the irony that, while along with Auden and Eliot, Dylan had changed the face of English poetry, he was the youngest to die.

There were more practical matters to consider urgently. Dylan had died intestate, so Caitlin and the children were facing destitution and funds had to be raised quickly – in the short term there were medical and funeral expenses to pay. Dylan's US publisher organised a committee on whose behalf leading literary figures such as E.E. Cummings, W.H. Auden, Arthur Miller and Tennessee Williams wrote appeal letters. It raised $20,000 (about £7,000 in 1953) within two months and the fund was eventually invested in a trust for the benefit of the family. A similar campaign was mounted by T.S. Eliot and Louis MacNeice in London and another in Swansea when Fred, Vernon, Dan Jones and other friends presented the American fundraisers' letter to the town's mayor, who started a local appeal.

Dan realised that Caitlin was in no fit state to manage her own affairs and after talking to David Higham and Stuart Thomas, Dylan's agent and Swansea solicitor respectively, arranged the necessary legal process to make her Dylan's sole heir. Due to the couple's hazy grip on finances, the poet's assets on death were valued at a paltry £100 – an under-estimation, as it turned out – but Caitlin also inherited the copyrights to his work. Her mental state was so fragile however, that the following day she went to stay with friends in London and after an evening's drinking tried to kill herself by jumping out of a third-floor window, the first of several suicide attempts after Dylan's death. Only a few weeks after leaving the psychiatric clinic in New York, she was back in another one in Surrey. She soon discharged herself and spent Christmas with Dan and Irene at the Boat House, where Dan was so disturbed by her violent and sexually provocative behaviour that he decided she – and the children – needed protecting from herself.

His discussions about Dylan's legacy with Higham and Stuart Thomas, who was also an old classmate of Dylan's, had also mooted the setting up of a trust to protect the future income from Dylan's copyrights for the family. The poet's death had boosted interest in his work even further, and the proceeds from *Under Milk Wood*, which was yet to be recorded by the BBC or published in print, were still to come. Dan felt there was no time to lose and before the year was out Caitlin had signed the deed that set up the trust, which would own the copyrights to the work for their duration: now seventy years in the UK. The revenue would be shared, with Caitlin entitled to 50 per cent during her lifetime, and the other 50 per cent divided equally between Llewelyn, Aeron and Colm. The money would be held in trust for them until they were adults, to protect their inheritance. Dan, David Higham and Stuart Thomas would be the trustees, with Dan taking responsibility for any editorial work that might be required to produce definitive versions of texts. The trustees had the best of motives but Dylan's financial legacy was to cause bitter disputes for years to come.

Dan's priority was to edit a final version of *Under Milk Wood*. Its first BBC broadcast, for which he also wrote the music, was scheduled for 25 January 1954. Richard Burton, who was now a lauded Shakespearean actor and Hollywood star, had been devastated by Dylan's death and took the poet's original part as First Voice, or narrator. Cast members dashed from the recording studio to a fundraising gala performance of an extract of the play at the Globe Theatre on Shaftesbury Avenue (now the Gielgud Theatre) on the night of the broadcast, with readings by Burton and Louis MacNeice, and a tribute from Edith Sitwell. All the proceeds, including the cast's fees, went to the memorial fund, raising £1,169.5s. When Caitlin was asked what Dylan would have thought about it, she replied that he would have liked the cheque. Ceri Richards designed the drop cloth and decor for the event, based on preparatory drawings and collages which incorporated herons, owls, blossom and the land and seascapes around Laugharne that, for him, Dylan had evoked so beautifully. The curtain, he explained, was in glorification of Dylan, and the stage decor more seriously suggested his passing and flight from the world. 'No one has read him with more love than I,' Ceri had written to Vernon on hearing of his death, and that feeling was expressed in many future works. Soon after Dylan died he suffered from a life-threatening illness himself and produced many drawings and collages incorporating motifs of life and death, and even Dylan himself. Dramatic paintings entitled 'Do not go gentle into that good night' portrayed a male figure tumbling from a white shroud held in the beak of an owl in flight.

Ceri's designs for the memorial event were shown soon after at a display at the Redfern Gallery and at a poetry reading Vernon took part in at the Glynn Vivian Art Gallery in Swansea. They were also used at a memorial service at the Royal Festival Hall in February that included a reading by Richard Burton of 'Fern Hill', the actress Edith Evans reading Edith Sitwell's tribute, the actor Michael Hordern reading Vernon's 'Elegiac Sonnet' in memory of his friend, and a recording of Dylan's rendering of 'And death shall have no dominion'. For Ceri, who was there, that was the perfect ending to a tribute which at times had left him unmoved.

The events were lost on the people of Laugharne. The BBC broadcast of *Under Milk Wood* was on the Third Programme (now BBC Radio 3), which did not reach the town that had inspired so many of the play's richly tragi-comic characters. The local Welsh service refused to repeat it on the grounds that it was not 'for family or home listening' – reflecting a chapel-influenced, puritanical streak in Welsh culture that can still dog those who want to celebrate Dylan's work to this day. The play, which sounded as fresh and original to British audiences as it had to New York ears, was a big success. When Dan's edited version was first published in 1954 it sold 53,000 copies and contributed to an income for the trust of £16,731 per annum in 1956–57 alone, far more than had been predicted.

One family member who did not benefit from the trust, however, was Dylan's mother, for reasons that are not clear. Her daughter Nancy's second husband had been paying the rent on the Pelican and providing her with £2 a week, but since he had married again she was living off social security. Soon after Dylan died she moved to the Boat House, which the trust bought from Margaret Taylor, to be near her grandchildren when they visited, and because she felt closer to her son there. But Caitlin's behaviour was so disturbing – 'screaming and shouting whenever she passed the hut, and staying out till all hours causing a scene' – that Florence retreated to the Pelican. From here she wrote in March to Ethel Ross, who lived with Fred, her brother-in-law, and her sister Mary. Ethel had invited her to a fundraising tribute to Dylan at Swansea Grammar School. Florence apologised for not being able to come as she had been in bed for a month suffering from nervous exhaustion and a heart condition. 'I still can't believe that I shan't see my boy any more,' she added. 'How I miss him I can never tell, to think in one year I lost my whole family, it's been a very severe blow, one I'm afraid I shall never really get over.'

As her health deteriorated, Florence went to stay with friends in Carmarthen, where Fred telephoned in October 1954 to ask if she would like to come and stay with the Janes family at the old farmhouse, Nicholaston Hall. He and Mary now had a baby daughter – me. 'I am looking forward to seeing your little daughter very much,' Florence wrote, '& what a sweet name (Hilary) you have chosen for her, & the boy too. I'm looking forward to seeing him as I have a very soft spot for little boys'. Florence was now living alone. Llewelyn and Aeron were at boarding school and often spent holidays with Caitlin's family, although their grandmother very much looked forward to the times when Aeron would stay with her. But Caitlin decided to leave the country, with funds provided by the trust. 'Caitlin went off to Elba yesterday ... she has taken Colm with her,' Florence's letter to Fred and Mary explained, 'so I do hope she behaves herself while she is there, but I'm afraid that is too much to expect'. She stayed away over Christmas, but didn't send presents to Aeron and Llewelyn.

It was the first of several visits to and from the Janeses. Fred drove the forty miles to Carmarthen to fetch her, and much to Ethel's surprise Florence stepped out of the car beaming, her pretty grey hair topped by a little black beret decorated with sparkles – most unusual at the time. It had come, she explained, in 'Caitlin's bundle from America' – a parcel of attractive clothes sent by well-wishers. She talked at length to Ethel about Dylan, who later turned their conversation into a dramatic monologue, in Florence's own words, written with understandable sympathy for the widow. A diary Ethel kept at the time, however, reveals her surprise at Florence's criticism of Caitlin. Although Ethel had always found Dylan's wife very stand-offish 'as if she was never really present ... Mrs Thomas made the most inhuman charges against her and has no pity.'

*Dylan's mother Florence Thomas, Fred and
baby Hilly at Nicholaston Hall c.1954*

Dylan was blameless in Florence's eyes. She had been very
concerned about him in his last years, when he was so breathless
he could barely walk the distance between the Boat House and
the Pelican, and had told his mother that he would die before her
when she asked him to look at papers that would concern him
after her own death. She reminisced fondly about how he always

had a pocketful of monkey nuts and sweets. 'I was picking the shells out of my chairs for months after he died. And sweets, the ones he didn't like, he'd put down the side of the chair. Dear boy! I wish I had him back.' But observant Ethel knew the other side of the story. 'We know of the escapades in London when Fred watched over him and kept him out of trouble. Poor Mrs Thomas disbelieves what Caitlin has taunted her with; his affairs in America and his intrigues at Oxford … poor Caitlin, the arch sinner, is villain of the piece. But we know some of Caitlin's difficulties and the awful state Dylan got into at Dan's in his later visits,' Ethel added darkly, 'so that once Dan thought he was going to die'.

Florence's thank-you note, like all those she sent, was heartfelt and full of questions about the children; Fred, whom she 'loved dearly'; and Dan and Vernon, both of whom had come to see Florence while she was visiting. 'All Dylan's friends are geniuses in their different ways,' she said, 'and I am so proud of them all'. She thanked Mary for looking after her as if she had been her own mother. 'You all made me feel so happy & at home. I love it with you, the children make me feel young & remind me of when mine were young and full of life & fun.' If Florence was not well enough to travel to Gower, they would correspond. She was delighted, she said, with a new edition of Dylan's short stories, *Quite Early One Morning*, that Dan sent her and which she read sitting up in bed.

The return of Caitlin from Elba in February 1955 filled her with dread, however. Probably unbeknown to Florence, she needed an abortion. 'I'm much happier when I don't see her,' Florence confided in Fred and Mary, 'although I am looking forward to seeing Colm, bless him. I hope she is kind to him as he is such a lovable little fellow & so like his father in ways, so is Aeron like Dylan in ways and looks, she is the only one with brown eyes'.

By June Florence had heard only once from Caitlin – but she had been contacted by Aeron's school, which wrote asking why the girl was the only pupil not in summer uniform. Florence arranged for the dresses to be sent to her from the Boat House so that she could make sure they were still suitable. Colm had been deposited at Blashford, while Caitlin was spending time with the cameraman who had recorded Dylan's second TV broadcast, but no one quite knew where.

It was the only hint that Florence gave of Caitlin's behaviour. Dan had been made aware, he said, of orgies at the Boat House, as had the local police. Florence was distraught. 'What a life she lives, what a shame, it's the children I feel sorry for & I feel mad she is still Dylan's widow, bless him, he is far better off dead than the husband of such a woman, if one can call her that.' She could not help commenting on how Caitlin had 'much too much money' in comparison to herself. Caitlin left for Rome in the spring of 1957, and according to Florence the family were going to live in America in the autumn as Llewelyn, or 'Welly' as the family nicknamed him, had won a place at Harvard, financed by the US trust. By the end of that year Florence's health was failing. She continued writing letters, signed 'Granny', with rows of kisses for Hilary and Ross and a ten-shilling note each as a Christmas present. Granny Thomas, as we knew her, died the following year. She sent her last letter on 20 June 1958, from the Boat House, where Dolly, the old home help, looked after her, as frequent heart attacks meant she was no longer well enough to be left alone. Florence remarked on how happy and well Aeron and Llewelyn had seemed on a recent visit. The weather was lovely and they spent most of their time rowing on the river in the family's boat.

Fred in his Gower studio, c.1960,
photographed by Peter Johns

Alfred Janes outside his home in Dulwich Village,
south London in 1966
photographed by Bernard Mitchell

CHAPTER SEVENTEEN
KEEPING THE SHOW ON THE ROAD

Perhaps the attention that Fred paid to Florence, whom he had known for twenty years, was his way of contributing to the welfare of his old friend's family. The upkeep of Nicholaston Hall was a big drain on his limited resources, and he was wise enough not to get involved with Dylan's posthumous financial affairs. Settling back into civilian life at the end of the war and deciding what and how to paint after such a long gap had been a challenge. In 1953 he painted a second self-portrait, aptly entitled *Puzzled*. He had moved on from still lifes to more figurative paintings with a satirical, slightly sinister edge. Their subject matter was often seaside scenes peopled by colourful, larger-than-life characters rather like those that inhabited some of Dylan's short stories such as 'Holiday Memory' – not that Fred would ever have admitted any direct influence.

Dan Jones, meanwhile, whose polymathic abilities did not stretch to dealing with all the administrative duties and decisions required of a literary trustee, was finding his role as a guardian of Dylan's estate a heavy burden. In May 1957 Caitlin had published the first of several angry confessional memoirs that she wrote about her life with Dylan, which did little to endear her to the trustees. At first the income from the trust had been eaten up not only by existing debts but by past creditors who had given up hope of ever receiving the money they were owed. Caitlin recognised herself that she needed to be kept on a tight rein and agreed to an allowance of £8 a week. The trustees received requests for top-ups of hundreds of pounds when she was in

Italy, and often complied although they were limited by strict foreign exchange controls.

Dan was also plagued by visitors, many of them American and sometimes in groups, who would turn up on his doorstep unannounced wanting to talk about Dylan Thomas. Those who were invited in often left with precious editions of Dylan's books, if left alone long enough to take them from his study. 'There was no time for my own work, and in any case I had no thought or energy to spare for it,' Dan complained. His livelihood was mainly dependent on completing commissioned works, but in the year that Dylan died, he did not complete anything, though his *Symphony No. 4, In memoriam Dylan Thomas*, was written the following year.

> At the end of two years my own family was almost in as great need as the Thomas family had been at the time of Dylan's death. The Thomas Estate, on the contrary was now like a ship well-launched and sailing always faster before a freshening wind. It was time for me to resign, and I did.

Dan had also been piqued by Kingsley Amis's comic 1955 novel *That Uncertain Feeling*, about a young librarian living in what was obviously Swansea, where Amis lectured at the university. Dan, whose co-trustee Stuart Thomas was a close friend of Amis's, was instantly recognisable as a bumptious Welsh composer called Stan Jones. He was replaced in 1957 as a trustee by Dylan's old Little Theatre acquaintance Wynford Vaughan Thomas, now a senior BBC journalist who had distinguished himself as a war correspondent while covering an air raid on Berlin from a Lancaster bomber and reporting from Belsen. He had felt honoured to be invited to become a trustee of a poet he admired so greatly, but twenty years later he admitted that he had been tempted to resign after countless baseless accusations by Caitlin about the trust's alleged mishandling of Dylan's estate – received through the firm of solicitors to whom the trust was paying £1,500 a year out of her share of its income. Dan, like many of Dylan's close friends, had also been dismayed by the publication in 1955 of John Malcolm Brinnin's memoir, *Dylan Thomas in America*. As Dylan's agent-cum-manager in the US, he had arranged most of the poet's engagements on his four tours of the country. The 15 per cent commission that he took was modest, though a welcome top-up to his income as a writer and university teacher. But given their length and the number of bookings, the tours were a huge undertaking that Brinnin mostly managed by remote control as Dylan criss-crossed the states for several months, often alone.

Brinnin was a genuine admirer of Dylan's work, eager to introduce it to wider, younger audiences, and deeply fond of the man – at least to begin with. But now he also needed to defend himself against accusations that promoting the performer at the expense of the poet had created a destructive vicious circle, and that Dylan had been encouraged to make a spectacle of himself in America for the entertainment of others. As Gwen put it: 'It might almost be said that he was killed partly by the grimace which responded to his entertainment and partly by the lack of any face which could see through it.' She also pointed out that the people whom Dylan had enthused about most – other poets – when he recounted his visits to his friends back home were almost entirely absent from Brinnin's book, while it spared little detail of the more self-destructive aspects of his behaviour in the last three years of his life, including his affairs with Americans Pearl Kazin, whom Brinnin called 'Sarah', and Liz Reitell. Only two years after Dylan's death, the revelations inflamed what Caitlin described as 'a still hot shovel of overloaded feeling'.

No one could have stopped Dylan from indulging in his excessive behaviour, but by arranging exhausting tours, accepting on his behalf countless invitations to social occasions which it would have been wiser to turn down, and conniving in his extra-marital affairs, Brinnin was not wholly innocent. Like Caitlin, he seemed to be able to live neither with nor without Dylan, but his claims that he and Reitell were 'circumstantial victims of an enchantment Dylan put upon anyone who came close to him,' and that 'no man was more adept in killing what he loved', were deeply distressing for his oldest friends. At least Brinnin allowed Caitlin to have her say: in a statement written at her request in *Dylan Thomas in America* she wrote that 'an intensive handful of months, at divided intervals, over a comparatively short number of years do not, however well recorded and with whatever honest intentions, do justice to the circumference of the subject'. Her plan to move to the US changed when she met an Italian, Giuseppe Fazio, and decided to move with her youngest child Colm to Sicily to live with him. Fazio was a strong character, who laudably tried – at first – to help Caitlin control her drinking and their relationship gave her some desperately needed personal stability. But it came at great cost, both financial and psychological, for her family and the trustees, which, at the time of writing, has not been entirely resolved.

Vernon Watkins, who was outraged by Brinnin's account, decided that the best response to Brinnin's book was to publish a collection of the many letters Dylan had written to him. With their personal insight into the painstaking effort that Dylan put into his craft, glimpses of his family life and struggle to earn a living, they would paint a very different picture. Their friendship was grounded in and nurtured by their mutual love of poetry, but on Vernon's part, at least, it was intensely personal. The year after Dylan died, Gwen had given birth to their fourth child, who was to have been his godson. The couple named him after their friend (as Ethel pointed out, since Dan Jones had done likewise, there were now so many Dylans they needed labels) and in the lovely early spring weather of that year, Vernon wrote a moving poem, 'Birth and Morning', for the godfather that would never meet his namesake.

I restore to the garden the footprints of one that was near
Whose arms would cradle you now, a magnanimous ghost,
But who sleeps without knowing your name in the turn and the
    quick of the year.

Vernon's publisher, T.S. Eliot at Faber, agreed to publish the letters. The trustees, however, who administered the copyright of Dylan's letters, would only grant permission if the book was brought out by Dylan's publisher, Dent, which had also produced Brinnin's book. Vernon was so reluctant to be associated with Brinnin that he refused. Eventually a very unusual compromise was reached in which Faber produced the book and Dent distributed it. In a hilarious over-reaction, Dent's lawyer was concerned, among other things, that Dylan's jokes about Fred's lack of letter writing might cause a libel suit. (The point that Fred would not have bothered to put pen to paper was seemingly lost on the lawyer.) Dylan's account of the Majoda shooting incident in New Quay caused protracted discussions. Vernon, who, like Dan, had no appetite for legal wrangling or the distraction from writing his own poetry, almost gave up.

When *Letters to Vernon Watkins* was eventually published in May 1957 it became an invaluable resource for biographers and students, but did not put a stop to Vernon's tribulations. He, too, was now so plagued by the Dylan fans who arrived uninvited at the bank to talk to him that he had to be moved away from the cashiers' desk. One day he brought home to Pennard a US steel magnate and his young bride, who had heard Dylan read and was making the pilgrimage on her honeymoon, trotting along the cliffs in high heels and an ankle bracelet. Fred was beyond the reach of casual visitors at the remote house in Nicholaston, but his sister-in-law Ethel described how researchers would ask to meet Fred, who treated every day as a working day and did not like to be interrupted, except for meals at set times. But some visitors would monopolise the day and expect meals

213

themselves, often arriving at the suggestion of Vernon, who had had enough of them himself in Pennard. Sometimes, on fine summer weekends, the Janes family would get up and leave the house for the beach to avoid them.

Fred did not want to sell his 1953 portrait of Dylan, despite several offers. But one American was very persistent – a representative of the Harry Ransom Research Center at the University of Texas at Austin. According to Ethel, he and his wife came to the house every day for a week in 1960 until Fred agreed to sell them the portrait. Dylan's manuscripts, papers and letters were all valuable collectors' items, many of which had been sold to American universities. Austin wanted to add to the portrait to their archive.

The day arrived for the painting to be collected from Nicholaston Hall and flown to Texas. A van drove up the quarter-mile-long drive to the house, and the driver brought in a large wooden box. Fred realised immediately that it was about three inches too wide all around. Mary's collection of *House & Garden* magazines were requisitioned and she and Fred set about crumpling up all the pages and packing them around the frame until Dylan looked as though he was surrounded by a beautiful coloured wreath. At last the box was loaded into the van, but when it set off down the drive, there was no mistaking the sound of falling masonry. It had taken a chunk out of one of the old dry stone walls that Fred had painstakingly restored. 'Goodbye Dylan,' he said as he finally waved the portrait off. 'Trouble till the last.'

Overseas interest in the work of Dylan and his contemporaries had mainly been confined to the US, but it was now growing in Italy, thanks to Roberto Sanesi, a leading Italian poet, critic, broadcaster and translator of, among others, Shakespeare, Yeats and T.S. Eliot. Sanesi had discovered Dylan's poetry as a young man and begun to translate it, but Dylan never read the letter that his admirer wrote to him before he died. Sanesi soon came to Wales to visit Dylan's birthplace, travelling by train from Milan with his belongings in a sailor's bag. He met both Vernon and Ceri Richards and his interest in Dylan's work grew to encompass theirs in a web of collaborations which included translations of poems from and into English, articles and books in Italian, including editions of Ceri's graphic work featuring illustrations of Vernon and Dylan's poetry.

Artists, poets and composers might have been paying tribute to Dylan in their own work, but ten years after his death there was still no memorial to the poet in his hometown. Visitors from around the world were surprised that Swansea had not honoured him in this way. One chilly January afternoon in 1963, Vernon found himself standing in front of a TV camera in Cwmdonkin Park making a gentle plea for such a tribute. The news travelled across the Atlantic and a few weeks later a telegram addressed simply to 'Vernon Watkins, Swansea', arrived at the bank. It was from the two women at Caedmon Records in New York who had recorded Dylan reading over a decade earlier and they wanted to help.

Vernon obtained permission to erect a stone in Cwmdonkin Park and Barbara Holdridge and Marianne Rooney were only too delighted to fund the memorial. The record label that they had launched as 22-year-olds with Dylan's reading in New York had made them audiobook pioneers and introduced his work and that of many other major poets to a generation that enjoyed unprecedented access to music and literature through vinyl records. 'If the cost is above fifty pounds, please don't hesitate to go ahead and have us billed,' they wrote with an American largesse that Swansea certainly lacked. Vernon chose a block of local sandstone with the help of another of Dylan's school contemporaries, Ronald Cour, a sculptor. Ron carved the last three lines of 'Fern Hill' into the stone, which they had found at Cwmrhydyceirw (pronounced coom-ree-dee-cai-rhoo) Quarry, just north of Swansea. It was unveiled on the tenth anniversary of Dylan's death. Some years later Vernon wrote two poems commemorating the tribute.

215

Caitlin Thomas, the poet's widow, with her daughter Aeronwy and son Colm in 1966 on their way to the High Court in London, where she sued for the return of the manuscript of Under Milk Wood

CHAPTER EIGHTEEN

NOT DYLAN THOMAS

By the time Dylan's memorial stone was unveiled, the Janes family were installed in their new home in south London. Dylan had been dead for ten years, but the aftermath of his death and its ramifications – financial, personal and cultural – seemed endless. While his work has inspired world-class artists, writers, musicians and performers of the highest order, from Richard Burton, Stan Tracey and George Martin to Bob Dylan, John Lennon and Peter Blake, he sometimes cast a long shadow over the lives of his oldest friends.

Fred had been teaching part time at the art school in Swansea and his opportunity to sell work had grown with the opening of the town's first commercial gallery in 1962, when four enterprising women created a showcase for modern Welsh artists at the Dillwyn Gallery, with the proud rallying cry that their output was as good as any to be found in the United Kingdom. The gallery's artists were offered a showcase by Kingsley Amis, who had left Swansea University after thirteen years to take up a fellowship at Cambridge. His marriage had broken up and his new partner, the glamorous novelist Elizabeth Jane Howard, was ill at ease with the close-knit Swansea set he had been part of – some of whom resented their thinly disguised caricatures in his satirical novels. But he remained friendly with Fred and included him in an exhibition of work by the Dillwyn's artists that he organised in Cambridge. Amis did not enjoy either the social or the academic life there, however, and moved to London after a couple of years, where he invited Fred and Mary to his famously boozy book launches.

Living in London again finally became a possibility for Fred, too, when he was offered a teaching post at Croydon College of Art in 1963. The chance to return to the capital, with its emerging experimental arts scene and access to national galleries like the Tate, was too good to miss. And the commercial opportunities available in London were obvious. Ceri Richards was achieving major success with retrospectives at the Whitechapel Art Gallery, renowned for its promotion of contemporary artists, and overseas at the Venice Biennale, where he won the prize for best painting in 1962. He had also been taken on by London's leading commercial gallery, Marlborough Fine Art. Dylan continued to inspire his work, notably in *Twelve Lithographs for Six Poems by Dylan Thomas*, full of powerful symbolic images of the cycle of nature. Mervyn Levy was in London too, making a name for himself as a writer, dealer and TV personality. Dan Jones and Vernon Watkins were now the only two members of Dylan's close circle who still lived in Swansea. Charlie Fisher lived in Canada, where he worked for the Canadian parliament transcribing proceedings, enjoyed the sophisticated social life that gave him access to, and drove a red Jaguar. Tom Warner had left for a post teaching music in south-east England.

Some of the first visitors to the Janeses' new home were Mervyn and Marie and their young son Ceri. Mervyn's 1950s TV series *Painting for Housewives*, the first programme to teach viewers to paint and draw, had raised his profile and he became a regular BBC broadcaster. His career as a prolific writer also took off and by the early 1960s he had written the first three of twenty-five books, including studies on modern artists like Henri Gaudier-Brzeska, Ruskin Spear, Carel Weight and, notably, L. S. Lowry, on whom he became a leading authority. As features editor of *Studio* magazine, Mervyn interviewed Salvador Dalí at his house in Spain and was spellbound by the surrealist's description of what would happen to his wife Gala's body after she died. 'Gala's flesh will be carefully pared from the bone, very finely minced, seasoned, sprinkled with powdered rhinoceros horn and eaten raw with a garnish of sea urchins. Her bones will be used to build a tower to her memory, supported with crutches, and embellished with bronze replicas of my moustaches.' It was *Under Milk Wood* on LSD. Dali promised to invite Mervyn to the feast but he waited in vain.

Mervyn's portraits of Dylan were also in demand but, mischievously, he often churned out new ones to meet it. He was also recognised for his support of artists through his skills as a dealer and curator, including his old friend Fred, whose work was now becoming less figurative and more abstract. In 1959 he had painted *Chirrup and Fruit*, named from the opening lines in the 'Prologue' that Dylan had written for his *Collected Poems*, and one of Fred's favourites. Petals, leaves, fruit and feathers are all visible but merge into an abstract welter of glowing sunset colours.

> This day winding down now
> At God speeded summer's end
> In the torrent salmon sun,
> In my seashaken house
> On a breakneck of rocks
> Tangled with chirrup and fruit

Before leaving Nicholaston Hall for London, a final task had been to collect bags of pale, fine sand from Oxwich beach that we washed in fresh water and sieved over and over again to remove the salt. In this next experimental phase, the sand was used in a relief effect and several of these works incorporated motifs and images from the sea shore or the flora and fauna of south-west Wales. Although Fred had distanced himself from his hometown and Dylan Thomas connections, the love of the natural world that they both shared was still visible in his work. Vernon was fascinated by Fred's versatility and in a BBC broadcast in 1962 remarked: 'Dylan Thomas would be amazed at the profusion of paintings that has emerged in these successive styles. In each phase of Alfred Janes's development there is an extraordinary meticulousness and mastery, at once recognisable as his own.' Once the mastery was complete, Fred would move on and try something else. It was challenging and exciting for him, but a gamble for anyone who tried to promote his work.

Competition was stiff on the London art scene, and Fred was aware of the pressure on Ceri to satisfy his dealer's demands at Marlborough Fine Art, who also represented Henry Moore, John Piper and younger talent like Patrick Caulfield and Allen Jones. The price of success, Fred suspected, was loss of independence, which he valued more highly than public recognition. He had, after all, seen Dylan pay a terrible price for that.

Mervyn persisted, however, by introducing Fred to London gallery owners. He was not a natural self-promoter, and like many artists suspicious of the cut-throat world of commercial dealers, but he knew at the age of fifty-five he had to somehow make his work more visible. In 1966 Mervyn jointly organised an important centenary exhibition called 'Metamorphosis – Figure into Abstraction' at the municipal Herbert Art Gallery and Museum in Coventry. Here Fred was again exhibiting alongside leading twentieth-century artists including Barbara Hepworth, Ben Nicholson, Victor Pasmore and John Piper. Ceri also encouraged him. He was now an influential figure in the art world as a trustee of the Tate and lecturer at the Royal College of Art. Anybody who was anybody in the art world went to Ceri's private views, including 'Basil Minto' – Cyril Connolly, Dylan's former editor at *Horizon*, whom he had lampooned in his still-unpublished *Death of the King's Canary* satire, and who was now chief book reviewer for the *Sunday Times*. Private views were important for making new contacts and the fun of rubbing shoulders with celebrities. Dylan and Fred's old friend William Scott's career was flourishing too and Mary went to the private view of his retrospective at the Tate in 1972. 'It's a good show, very painterly, extremely beautiful handling of paint,' she wrote to Ethel, adding that she had spotted 'Hockney all peroxided and green velvet suited'. Just as stimulating were the 'happenings' in swinging London. The Institute of Contemporary Arts' inaugural exhibitions in its Regency building in The Mall, for example, caused quite a stir with a waxwork model of a dead hippie, computers, pulsing TV screens and a mosaic floor made of coloured light. In 1968, this was revolutionary.

Personal ties with Swansea were still strong. Vernon came to stay in Dulwich when he was in London to give readings and talks, and see exhibitions of Fred's work. After retiring from the bank he took up a prestigious Gulbenkian Fellowship in Poetry at Swansea University, and was awarded an honorary doctorate in literature. Everyone who came to the house would be offered a visit to the Dulwich Picture Gallery, just over the road, with its exquisite collection of Old Masters. Gwen recalled her tour with Vernon. 'It was such an experience because Fred was an innovative painter but you could see how much he loved some of these pictures, in the way that Vernon and Dylan loved Yeats and Blake – they nourished them.'

Some requests for visits to Dulwich were not so welcome, however. Academics or journalists requesting interviews with Fred were often turned down if they wanted to talk about Dylan. A private collector who asked Fred if he could identify the subject of a painting – a 1950s study of an unnamed man – got a quick-fire reply: 'Not Dylan Thomas.' TV companies that wanted to film him talking about his own work needed strong powers of persuasion and Mary's patient coaxing to get him in front of their cameras. His work and that of Dylan Thomas could speak for itself as far as he was concerned.

Vernon was soon to follow in Dylan's footsteps with a trip to America when Theodore Roethke, a Pulitzer Prize winner and

Professor of Poetry at Washington State University in Seattle, invited him to replace him while he took a sabbatical. Now that Vernon had retired from the bank he took up the offer, and in 1967 he and Gwen departed for Seattle with the three youngest of their five children. Two weeks later I rushed into the kitchen to tell my parents about a news item the BBC had just broadcast. 'Mum, Dad, Vernon is dead,' I blurted out, lacking the maturity to break the news more sensitively. Their reaction was one of total horror. Fred was devastated at the news that only two weeks after arriving in the US, Vernon had collapsed and died aged sixty-one of a heart condition while playing his beloved tennis. 'This terrible news of Vernon has shaken us all. Fred is in a daze,' Mary wrote to Ethel. Gwen was now left a widow with a large family to support, and in reply to Fred and Mary's letter of condolence, she said that she had twice gone on to the tennis court to tell Vernon to stop playing, as they knew he had a heart condition. 'He died as he lived,' she wrote, 'getting his own way'. His ashes were brought back to Pennard and interred in the church there, where a memorial is inscribed with lines he wrote in memory of Dylan:

Death cannot steal the light which love has kindled,
Nor the years change it.

By the time he died, Vernon had published seven volumes of poetry with Faber. At Hunt's Bay, a rocky cove below the bungalow where he lived and wrote, a small granite stone is inscribed with lines from his poem about an ancient Celtic bard, 'Taliesin in Gower':

I have been taught the script of stones,
and I know the tongue of the wave.

The Times reported that Vernon was being considered as a replacement for John Masefield as Poet Laureate at the time of his death, alongside Robert Graves, Cecil Day Lewis, Edmund Blunden and John Betjeman. 'In many ways it would have been a happy choice,' the paper said, 'at once a tribute to Celtic genius and to a poet of unusual humility'. Vernon's poetry is still read and revered. Rowan Williams, the former Archbishop of Canterbury, recently described him as one of the twentieth century's most brilliant and distinctive voices.

The loss of Vernon ended another cherished friendship for Fred. There would be no more visits for Sunday tea at their bungalow, 'The Garth', during the holidays that the Janes family spent in Gower – sometimes twice a year. Only a few years later, the circle shrank again when Ceri died aged sixty-eight in 1971, on the anniversary of Dylan's death on 9 November. Benjamin Britten, for whose opera *Noye's Fludde* Ceri had designed the original costumes and animal masks, accompanied Peter Pears in songs from Schubert's *Winterreise*, one of Ceri's favourite pieces, at his memorial service. In his obituary for *The Times*, Pears said that Ceri 'was one of the most gifted British artists of the past fifty years'. Ten years after his death Ceri was honoured with a retrospective at the Tate, and when a gallery named after him was opened at Swansea University in 1984, Fred wrote in the catalogue:

> He was a wonderful friend. His modesty regarding his work and his kindness were legendary ... suffice it to say that if of all the things you have seen and heard, felt, touched and tasted in this miraculously rich world there were some you loved the most, and that one man created quite a few of those, then you owe him a great debt.

This left Dan Jones as the last of Dylan's creative circle living in Swansea. By the mid-1960s he was writing his sixth symphony and had composed many string quartets and sonatas. Dan often stayed in Dulwich when he visited London for performances of his work, such as his first opera, *The Knife*, which received its premier at Sadler's Wells. He conducted at the Albert Hall and the Proms, and recorded commissions from the BBC and the Royal Philharmonic Orchestra in the capital's studios. But when he phoned Fred one evening to talk about the 'Dylan case', which had been reported in the papers, Fred asked: 'What case?'.

It was the first of many legal actions in a never-ending battle over the rights and ownership of Dylan's work. Caitlin wanted the manuscript of *Under Milk Wood* that Dylan had left in a London pub before leaving for the US for the last time. Douglas Cleverdon, the BBC producer who had found and kept it as a grateful Dylan said he could, had sold the manuscript, which was now owned by the Times Book Company. *Under Milk Wood*, whose genesis Cleverdon had nurtured for years, had been reprinted many times and earned tens of thousands in royalties. While the Dylan Thomas Trust owned the rights, the manuscript was a valuable object in itself. Caitlin claimed that Cleverdon had not been the rightful owner and had no right to sell it, and that the manuscript belonged to Dylan's estate. She lost the case in the High Court in London and had to the pay costs herself. Mary bought *The Times* to read the coverage after Dan's phone call, but Fred took no interest in it whatsoever.

Caitlin was on the warpath. Two months later she turned on the trustees and sued them for withholding money from the sale of some of Dylan's letters to an American magazine. In 1963 David Higham, Dylan's former agent and now a trustee, had received a long letter from her saying that she had noticed she was putting on weight and was very surprised, aged forty-nine, to have given birth to a baby boy, Francesco. He was Giuseppe Fazio's illegitimate son – and she wanted the child to be made a beneficiary of the trust. The trustees managed rights to Dylan's work carefully, only allowing new work that came to light to be published in titles by him, rather than anthologies. It also granted Caedmon Records exclusive rights to their high quality US recordings of his work, thus benefiting the estate, who got the royalties, and Caedmon, who dominated the audio market for Dylan's work. As a result of its stewardship, the trust's income was growing steadily, although Fazio was never aware of its true worth, as Caitlin kept this hidden from him. He suspected as much and eventually the trustees agreed to hand over her share in full. Now, instead of Caitlin's three children by Dylan sharing 50 per cent of its income, she wanted Francesco to be included and their half to be divided into four. The trustees declined, and in any case they had little room for manoeuvre because of the way the trust had been set up. Llewelyn and Aeron also disagreed, although Colm was still too young to have a say.

Caitlin had received £5,500 as her share of the trust's income the year before Francesco's birth, as well as personal royalties from a Broadway play partly based on her book about Dylan. A self-confessed alcoholic, she wanted more money to fund her rackety, drink-fuelled lifestyle in Rome and Sicily. One weekend she served more than ten writs with different causes of action on Stuart Thomas, the trust's lawyer. The crisis was averted when she was a passenger in a car caught by police driving the wrong way up a one-way street in Rome and hit one of the officers. She ended up in custody and Stuart Thomas flew to Rome to get her out. With the backing of Aeron and Llewelyn, he persuaded her to drop the costly but pointless litigation on which she was throwing money away – money supplied, of course, from the trust and much of it going to her own (very expensive) solicitors. In the early 1970s she overcame her addiction to alcohol and lost her appetite for legal challenges. But there were more bitter battles ahead between Dylan's children and Caitlin's son Francesco over his claim for a share of the estate.

Aeronwy Thomas Ellis, the poet's daughter, c.1976

CHAPTER NINETEEN

FAMILY MATTERS

The Thomas children had scattered after the death of their father and Caitlin's departure for Italy. Llewelyn went to Harvard, Aeron was at boarding school in England, while Colm lived with Caitlin in Sicily and Rome, where Giuseppe Fazio worked in the film industry and they had an apartment. But the family spent some holidays together in Sicily, and one summer Aeron invited a friend, Fiona Nicholls (now Green), to go with her. They were both pupils at Dartington Hall in Devon, a liberal, progressive co-educational boarding school where almost nothing was compulsory, but according to Fiona, both girls felt like fish out of water and bonded over their mutual unhappiness. Caitlin valued strong female friendships – she was close to her sisters and several other women – and wanted the same for Aeron, so she invited Fiona for a summer holiday in Sicily. It was a brutal awakening for the fifteen-year-old.

'Caitlin was the most gorgeous woman, beautiful and talented, but she drank like there was no tomorrow and the virago would take over,' Fiona says. 'Your eyes would see one thing but your ears would hear something else. She was very good to me, but as a mother she was hell on wheels.' Fazio drank less than Caitlin, but he was a violent, controlling man who could 'erupt like a volcano' and frequently lashed out at her. Once, when Fiona tried to intervene, she caught the force of his blow instead. He also tried, unsuccessfully, to get the teenager to sleep with both him and his brother. Nothing was said, and in any case Fiona knew that Caitlin would have been livid if she had found out. Aeron, according to her friend, was like the rock that held them all together.

During the holiday, Fiona fell for Llewelyn, a gentle, sensitive young man who was about to leave for Harvard and 'as pure and innocent as if he had just jumped out of the egg'. While Fiona remained friends with Aeron, she and Llewelyn lost touch after he went to America, only seeing him occasionally in London, where Fiona lived in Fitzrovia with her husband and children. But forty years later, she and Llewelyn met again and spent the last years of his life together, when he preferred to be known as Thomas Llewelyn. Fiona is an artist and psychotherapist and her insight into the effect on the Thomas children of their upbringing is revealing. After leaving Harvard, Llewelyn became a successful copywriter at the J. Walter Thompson advertising agency in London, where his anarchic creative spirit and wit endeared him to his colleagues. But he disliked being asked about his background and after marrying Rhiannon, the stepdaughter of Stuart Thomas, his father's former solicitor and one of the estate's trustees, he relocated to work for the agency in Australia, where they had a daughter, Jemima – the eldest of Dylan's grandchildren. The couple divorced and Llewelyn returned to England and became a gardener.

Llewelyn described his prolonged stays in Hampshire with Caitlin's family as 'paradise' to Fiona, and hated it when they came to take him away or it was time to go back to boarding school. Dylan never travelled with his family, even if they were on the same train. The constant abandonment by his parents took its toll on the boy. As well as suffering from asthma, he was extremely nervous, had all sorts of phobias and fears and controlled himself and other people in order to cope. 'Never apologise, never explain,' was his motto, according to Fiona. Like his parents he drank too

228

much, and like his father he thought it made him better company. Dylan, who liked to bet on horse races, had introduced Llewelyn to gambling when he sent him off to the betting shop with the slips. But Llewelyn was a far more successful gambler than his father and once, according to Fiona, gave her half the proceeds when he put £8 on an accumulator – a run of races in which he predicted the winners – and won £30,000. He even kept a diary of all the horses that he backed, illustrated with cartoons.

Llewelyn also shared Dylan's passion for thrillers, Agatha Christie especially, and wrote them himself in secret. But when Fiona pointed out the connection, he retorted that it had nothing to do with his father. He had never read anything about Dylan until Fiona lent him a couple of biographies – but that, he said, only made him hate his father as well as his mother. He had fallen out with Caitlin's partner, Giuseppe Fazio, on a visit to Italy, after which Caitlin wrote and told him that she no longer wanted anything to do with him. He showed her letter to Fiona. 'It was cold and dense,' she says, 'and though Llewelyn projected a tough, stoic exterior, underneath he was devastated. He wanted her to be a mother. It was so sad.'

Although Colm could not even remember his father, he never really came to terms with his background either. Caitlin took him to Italy with her but sent him back to England to attend boarding school and live with his grandmother and aunts in Hampshire, as Llewelyn had done. But Colm left at eleven and completed the rest of his schooling in Rome. With his mop of blond curls and blue eyes, Colm had always been the baby of the family, but the arrival of his half-brother Francesco changed that. Like Llewelyn, he distanced himself from his roots, following him to Australia, where he graduated from Canberra University. He too divorced his first wife, but married for a second time. Colm eventually settled in the Abruzzo region east of Rome, where Caitlin had built a house with the proceeds of the US trust fund. A charming, sociable but restless soul who liked a drink, he had a series of jobs, buffered partly by his share of the income from the trust – on average about £8,000 a year.

Whether they like it not, the children of writers, artists and musicians are future guardians of their parents' creative legacy, and given the detachment of her two brothers, it fell to Aeron to pick up the mantle of her famous father. But Caitlin rarely talked about Dylan, and the children knew little about him. Aeron did not read any of his poetry until she was in her twenties and invited to give a public reading of 'Fern Hill'. It was a revelation. 'It was so familiar – his lyrical take on these places I knew. I could see it all in my mind's eye.' She felt the same about *Under Milk Wood* when she read that soon afterwards, especially as so many of its forty characters, like Ocky Milkman and Polly Garter, who loved having babies, were based on the Laugharne townsfolk of her childhood.

Aeron had finished her schooling in Italy, and then trained as a nurse in London. But she returned to Rome, where she worked in PR and as a journalist on the *Daily American* – and fell in love with an Italian man. When the relationship broke up some years later, she came back to England. The little girl who had resented being labelled as 'Dylan Thomas's daughter' graciously grew into the role, for which there was now a big demand. One evening Mary travelled across London to St John's Wood ('hell of a journey – rail go slow') to hear Aeron and Mervyn reading Dylan's work. 'Mervyn reads excellently and is quite an actor and has a good voice and of course genuinely likes the poems,' Mary wrote to Ethel. 'He knows how to win an audience – amusing, humble and slightly arrogant too. Aeron's voice is very light and it is difficult to accustom oneself to it after hearing Dylan booming away. She read the prose very well.' Petite and pretty with a mass of curls and big brown eyes, Aeron reminded everyone of Dylan. And her charm and impish sense of humour echoed the qualities in her father that had made him so lovable.

Mary often entertained family friends with a 'wicked Welsh tea' – a spread of dainty sandwiches, scones and Victoria sponge – a sit-down affair around the kitchen table, laid with a proper cloth and her best china. Aeron came one afternoon with Mervyn, Marie and Ceri, and as we played football in the garden afterwards, Mervyn entertained us with his impression of Toulouse-Lautrec, the dwarf painter (political correctness was yet to be invented). Donning an old trenchcoat which came to the ground when he knelt, and my school boater as a hat, he waddled around the garden muttering in a ridiculous French accent.

In the garden at the Janeses' house in London c.1971 –
from left: Aeronwy Thomas, Mary Janes, Mervyn and
Marie Levy, with their son Ceri in the foreground

Mervyn was still an imposing figure, despite his own lack of height, and Fred made a final portrait of him fifty years after the first award-winning painting. After Marie's death Mervyn continued to visit Fred and Mary in Dulwich, and before he died in 1996, posed with Fred at the kitchen sink for a reprise of the photo that had been taken of them washing up in Redcliffe Street fifty years earlier.

Fred and Mervyn Levy in Fred's London home in the 1980s
in a reprise of the 1930s photo taken at their London digs

In 1970 Aeron was invited to accompany the Pendyrus Male Choir, one of Wales's finest, on a promotional tour of the US. One of its members, Trefor Ellis, knew nothing of Dylan Thomas, but he was one of the choir's younger singers who found Aeron very attractive. Trefor came from the south Wales mining town of Pontypridd and worked in the pits as a measuring boy, assessing how much coal the miners had cut on their shift. It was a world away from Aeron's upbringing, but singing and the spoken word, twin pillars of culture in south Wales, brought them together.

As the US tour progressed, Trefor enjoyed listening to stories like 'The Outing', which reminded him of his own childhood trips to the seaside. It was only when he noticed at one reading in the US that two American nuns were listening to Aeron reading 'Fern Hill' with tears pouring silently down their cheeks that the power of her father's poetry sank in. By the time they arrived back in the UK, Trefor and Aeron were a couple. Learning to fit in with the 'Thomas dynasty', as he calls Aeron's extended family, wasn't easy. When Colm telephoned one day to speak to Aeron, he asked his sister why an Indian man had answered the phone. 'No,' Aeron replied, 'it's a Welshman from Pontypridd'.

Trefor first met Caitlin, or 'Mother', as they called her, at the premier of the film of *Under Milk Wood* in 1972. Filmed on location in Fishguard in Pembrokeshire, its stellar cast was led by Richard Burton, who again took the part of First Voice. Peter O'Toole played Captain Cat and Burton's then wife, Elizabeth Taylor, was dead Rosie Probert, 'the one love of his sea life that was sardined with women'. Arranging for these three leading Hollywood stars to coincide in Fishguard was, the director Andrew Sinclair recalled, like fixing a weekend between Howard Hughes, Elizabeth II and Puck. Leading Welsh actors like Glynis Johns, Siân Phillips and the young Angharad Rees (a childhood friend of Aeron's) were also cast members.

Caitlin made a rare return trip to England for the event, accompanied by what Trefor describes as 'the Italian set'. He was careful to remain detached from the trust's affairs and any family quarrels, so Caitlin saw the good-natured Welshman as a calming influence and was always very kind to him. Her own life was becoming more serene, though the absence of drink played almost as important part in her life as its presence had. Instead of a second home, pubs became places to avoid, but Caitlin would always comment on what was in everyone else's glass. She even wrote a memoir, *Double Drink Story*, published posthumously, about how alcohol had ruined her life with Dylan. Trefor felt less at ease with Caitlin's sister Nicolette Devas and her family. 'They were artists. It was a different world. I worked in the mines and had lived a life of poverty. It was only when they realised that I could sing that they accepted me.'

Trefor was more at home with a very different artist. 'Fred was very kind. I came up from the valleys and I was lost, but he welcomed me with open arms.' While some people looked down on Trefor, Fred accepted him for who he was and took an interest in his background – as Dylan and Vernon surely would have too. Trefor was taken aback by Fred's latest work, however. This was the era of Labour Prime Minister Harold Wilson's so-called 'white heat of technology', which was expected to transform Britain's economy. Artists were developing early twentieth-century ideas about 'ready-made' art by artists like Marcel Duchamp, and making work from mass-produced objects. Fred, who now described himself as a 'maker of pictures' rather than a painter, was making constructions using found materials like shattered windscreen glass, raiding my collection of marbles and experimenting with industrial materials like PVA and perspex. 'Most of what I have done has come out of this love of materials and tools and methods,' he wrote in the catalogue for his 1974 Welsh Arts Council retrospective at their new gallery in Cardiff. 'To me, craft is just doing things well and it is craft that we try to put into our work. Art is something that other people do or do not get out of it.' Trefor found this idea challenging at first. 'How can you have art with marbles?' he wondered when he saw Fred's constructions. 'On reflection I think it was very brave,' he says now.

When Trefor and Aeron got married in London in 1973, we all went to the wedding. Trefor's Pendyrus choir friends sang at the ceremony; Colm gave Aeron away and Fred was a witness. At the

234

Chelsea Arts Club reception afterwards, the Bohemian contingent of Aeron's circle made an interesting mix with Trefor's friends and family from the valleys, several of whom were deaf and communicated through sign language.

If Aeron still felt any anger towards her parents she had learned to live with it and love her father's work instead. She began to translate Italian poetry and write it herself. Her first volume, *Later Than Laugharne*, was published in 1976 with a foreword by Mervyn. 'Aeron loved giving readings and she loved meeting other poets and going to literary festivals,' Trefor says. This was complemented by studying for a degree in English literature and comparative religion. (Lacking practical skills, she had made a hopeless nurse, according to Trefor.) A deeply religious woman, Aeron had started off a Catholic, then flirted with Zen Buddhism, but finally converted to Anglicanism, and her faith certainly helped her overcome her turbulent childhood. She and Trefor attended the church near the home where he still lives in south-west London – and of course he sings in its choir.

Thomas's grave in Laugharne, Wales

CHAPTER TWENTY

TIME PASSES

Not long after Aeron and Trefor married she suggested that he sing some Welsh songs to add variety to a reading. The event was a success and they often performed together after that, notably at the launch of the Dylan Thomas Society in Swansea in 1977 – the brainchild of Dan Jones and Ronald Cour, the sculptor who had carved Dylan's memorial stone in Cwmdonkin Park. The founding of the society and the publication that year of Dan's memoir, *My Friend Dylan Thomas*, aimed to foster serious interest in Dylan's literary achievements, as opposed to other aspects of his life. Dan's own output continued to be prodigious. As well as numerous chamber and orchestral works, including the music for the investiture of the Prince of Wales in 1969, by 1985 he had completed his twelfth symphony. A thirteenth was completed the year before he died while composing at his desk in 1993.

Dylan's literary legacy received a boost from an unexpected quarter – the US President, Jimmy Carter. Dylan was his favourite poet, and on a tour of the UK in the summer of 1977, he visited Poets' Corner in Westminster Abbey, where great British writers from Chaucer to Ted Hughes are commemorated. Carter expressed his hope that Dylan would one day have his own memorial there. Caitlin wrote from Rome to the White House to express her surprise and appreciation. 'I would like to see my husband buried in Westminster,' she said. 'What had his way of life to do with the merit of his writing?'

The Welsh slate stone, inscribed with the last two lines of 'Fern Hill', was eventually unveiled in Westminster Abbey on 1 March – St David's Day – in 1982. Dylan is flanked by George Eliot and Lord Byron, with Gerald Manley Hopkins and Henry James near neighbours. When the family arrived for the ceremony they were amazed at the queue around the abbey, according to Trefor. Aeron took part in the ceremony along with two of Dylan's grandchildren – her eldest child, Huw, aged seven and Llewelyn's fifteen-year-old daughter, Jemima, who laid daffodils on the plaque. Four hundred guests – including the poet and then president of the Dylan Thomas Society, Ted Hughes, and Michael Foot, then Labour Leader of the Opposition – listened to readings of 'Fern Hill' and 'Poem in October'. The anniversary of Dylan's death is still marked each year with the laying of a wreath on the plaque.

Jimmy Carter honoured Dylan again twenty years later when he opened the Dylan Thomas Centre in the old dockside area of Swansea, one of Dylan's stamping grounds in his cub reporter days, which was gradually being redeveloped as a 'maritime quarter' with new waterside property developments, cafes and cultural centres. One of these is the Dylan Thomas Theatre, opened in 1983 as a permanent home for the Swansea Little Theatre and named after its most famous member. The Dylan Thomas Centre houses a permanent exhibition about the poet and hosted in 1998 the first Dylan Thomas Festival, now an annual event to mark his birthday. It came as a surprise to some in Swansea that Carter, a deeply religious teetotaller, held Dylan in such high esteem. Many local people – including councillors and tourism officials – were more likely to write him off as a hell-raising drunk than appreciate his literary achievements, and were slow to catch on to his potential as a cultural asset for the city.

A notable guest returned to Swansea to give the address at the Dylan Thomas Society's annual dinner on the fiftieth anniversary of Dylan's death in 2003 – Charlie Fisher. His early promise as a poet, noted in his days as a *South Wales Evening Post* reporter, was fulfilled in the 1980s with a critically acclaimed volume, *The Locust Years*. As a parliamentary recorder in Canada he had been able to travel widely in the summer recess, but in the early 1960s, he chose caves rather than hotel beds as a guest of the gypsy population around Granada. Here he learned to play flamenco guitar, speak the dialect and live as one of the family. The caves were destroyed in 'a cloudburst of biblical intensity' one night, and eventually the gypsy way of life as he knew it disappeared.

Charlie recorded his life with the gypsies in an unpublished memoir, *Adios Granada* (you can read extracts on a website about his life and work). 'They know very well', he wrote, 'that in their situation material things are only acquired at the cost of something they prize infinitely more, namely a certain freedom – freedom to move about, freedom not to have a "regular job" and freedom not to have a boss.' It was an aspiration Dylan and many of his creative Swansea friends shared. Charlie was almost ninety when he made the speech at the Dylan Thomas Centre, but he still knew how to make an entrance. In a midnight blue Armani jacket, still handsome and erect, his hair tied back in a ponytail, he looked, according to one guest, like a cross between Timothy Leary and Geronimo. In later life he had explored Mexico, India, Morocco and the Far East – where he died in Bangkok in 2006.

Aeron's support for the cultural institutions inspired by Dylan's work and her willingness to act as an ambassador for Swansea and Laugharne was unstinting, but the effort eventually took its toll. While she was pregnant with her second child, Hannah, in 1978, she suffered a haemorrhage and was diagnosed with polycythemia, a type of leukaemia that causes the over-production of red blood cells. Chemotherapy tablets helped, but Aeron tired easily and suffered from three more bleeds, which seemed to coincide with stressful times. One of them was in the mid-1990s, when the trustees of Dylan's estate faced another bout of legal action by Caitlin's Italian son, Francesco Fazio.

Caitlin had been living a quieter life in Sicily, returning only on special occasions such as the unveiling in 1984 of a blue plaque commemorating Dylan's stay at the house in Delancey Street. 'It is with mixed feelings of my wonderful Bohemian past and my present dull attempt at respectability, being a model of squaredom, that I place this plaque on our once worldly living and loving home, in loving memory of my irreplaceable Dylan,' were her words as she unveiled the plaque, *The Times* reported. Two years later she was back for the publication of her memoir *Caitlin: A Warring Absence* in 1986. *People* magazine dispatched a reporter to interview her in her villa in Sicily to mark the event. He found her frail and withdrawn at seventy-two, swallowing vitamin pills after every meal, while Giuseppe Fazio was genial and loquacious. The journalist asked him if he was fazed by following in the footsteps of Dylan Thomas. 'Intimidated by Dylan Thomas? Me?' he said. 'Not at all. I am intimidated by Sophocles, Homer, Virgil, Thucydides and the rest. Remember, there is nothing new under the sun.'

'Except Dylan Thomas,' Caitlin added.

She lived on for forty years without Dylan, dying in 1994 aged eighty. At her request (and a cost of £10,000 to the trust), her body was brought back to Wales to be buried alongside Dylan's in Laugharne. After Stuart Thomas, who had been a trustee since the outset, died the following year, Francesco Fazio tried to resurrect his claim as a beneficiary of the trust. Caitlin had left everything to him in her will, including her share of the house in Abruzzo, which she jointly owned with him, Aeron and Colm. But her 50 per cent share of the trust's income passed to Llewelyn, Aeron and Colm, and now Francesco claimed a share too, backdated from the beginning. It was worth having – in 1990-91 alone the trust's income was in excess of £90,000. But if he won, the trust would be bankrupt and his half-siblings personally liable for his share.

In a surprising turn of events, Kingsley Amis had taken over in 1986 as a trustee from an ailing Wynford Vaughan Thomas, who died the following year. It was the same year that Amis's Booker prize-winning novel, *The Old Devils*, appeared. He was a long-standing friend of Stuart Thomas from his days as a lecturer at Swansea University, but the book lampooned his Welsh cronies whose social lives revolved around booze and the Mumbles Yacht Club (open when the pubs shut), with Dylan thinly disguised as 'Brydan' and Wynford a likely candidate for the womanising TV presenter who trades on being a professional Welshman. Stuart Thomas took it all in his stride, while Wynford, like some other locals who recognised themselves, was not so amused.

A few years later, Amis made a more personal attack in his memoirs on Dylan, whom he met on only one occasion, when he was disappointed not to be treated to the 'pub performance' that he expected. He described Dylan 'an outstandingly unpleasant man, one who cheated and stole from his friends and peed on their carpets', belittled his literary achievements and didn't even try to conceal his contempt for Caitlin and Dan Jones. Amis's opinion of Dylan must have contributed to the tarnishing of his posthumous reputation, but the rationale for appointing the novelist as a trustee was his knowledge of the literary world and his standing in it, attributes which made him a valuable advisor on the protection of Dylan's literary estate. Bruce Hunter, the literary agent who took over from David Higham after his death in 1978, found that a day rarely went by without dealing with Dylan's copyrights in the thirty years that he managed them.

Under Milk Wood was perennially successful, not just as a drama to perform or a text for study on the English syllabus, but as an inspiration for musicians like the late jazz pianist Stan Tracey, resident pianist at Ronnie Scott's famous Soho showcase. On the night bus home he apparently dreamt up his haunting jazz suite, named after the play and recorded in 1965. Twenty years later it was the Beatles' producer, George Martin, who recorded his own interpretation of *Under Milk Wood*. The project was the brainchild of a Carmarthenshire-based publisher who had spotted a note by Dylan on a manuscript of the play suggesting that he intended to add more songs and music. Martin's cast was as stellar as the original film version's, with First Voice read by Anthony Hopkins, who comes, like Richard Burton, from Port Talbot. Martin set more of the text to music and performers like Elton John, Tom Jones, Mark Knopfler and Bonnie Tyler took part.

Thanks in part to the trustees, who since 1986 now included Michael Rush – a lawyer, former chief of West Glamorgan County Council and one of the Bristol Channel Yacht Club crowd based in Mumbles – Dylan's heirs were benefiting from an income that was steadily growing, even after the agents had taken their 10 per cent cut and the trustees claimed expenses, such as travel to meetings and business lunches in London, usually at the Garrick or Carlton clubs. Following complaints from Caitlin that Stuart Thomas was abusing his entitlement to expenses, he was called before the Law Society (the professional governing body for lawyers), but completely exonerated.

For a poet, such an increase in their income after death is probably unprecedented, and Francesco Fazio, who had been very close to his mother and supported her in her old age, was determined to share that legacy. The original deeds setting up the trust in 1953 had been replaced in 1957 when the Inland Revenue demanded a proper valuation of the estate. The tax authority had noticed that the trust had received £47,000 in copyright fees in the three years since its launch, which voided the original paltry valuation of Dylan's assets at £100 when he died. An amendment was made to the trust to reflect this increase in value, and Francesco Fazio's claim rested on whether wording in the original document stating that Caitlin would share the income with 'all my children' could apply to her illegitimate son by another man.

It took seven long years for the dispute to be settled. Michael Rush, who was by now the only remaining trustee, dealt with the litigation. Llewelyn, who had been reunited with Fiona Green again at Caitlin's funeral and was living with her in Devon, represented the family, despite his reluctance to be associated with his father. It was a very distressing time for Aeron, who had suffered another major bleed, sufficiently serious to need treatment in intensive care. The High Court eventually dismissed the case in 2002, but the relief at having won was tempered by the legal bill. The family was awarded costs of £70,000, but as Fazio had no money, the Thomases had to pay them. Fortunately Michael Rush had put aside a 'fighting fund' of £40,000 from royalties, but the children had to provide the remaining £30,000. Despite the strain of the litigation, Aeron kept up her role as an ambassador for the Dylan Thomas estate, and a writers' champion as president of the Alliance of Literary Societies, as well as writing and performing her own poetry. Her generous nature meant she sometimes over-committed herself, but one event she agreed to read at was not to be missed – a celebration of Fred's life and work.

If ever anyone raged against the dying of the light it was Fred. The setbacks of old age were frustrating for a man who was remarkably fit, had eaten a healthy diet (his morning porridge mixed with All Bran and chopped apple was a daily fixture) and kept extremely active mentally. His last works were masterly reworkings of pictures from his 1960s abstract 'liquid oil' period. Some of the original swirling shapes, lines and flecks remained, but the paintings were reborn as more figurative still lifes and dream-like seascapes reminiscent of the Gower coastline. The day before he was admitted to hospital with kidney failure in January 1999, he sent me on an errand to buy the finest paintbrush I could find. He died aged eighty-seven on 3 February.

One of Fred's favourite poems by Dylan was 'Prologue' – the work that he had written as an introduction to the best-selling *Collected Poems*. When Fred had reluctantly written a short article about Dylan thirty years earlier, he opened it with these lines from the poem.

> ....I hack
> This rumpus of shapes
> For you to know
> How I, a spinning man,
> Glory also this star, bird,
> Roared, sea born, man torn, blood blest.
> Hark: I trumpet the place
> From fish to jumping hill!

He chose the lines because they expressed for him so fully the sum of his memories of Dylan Thomas. The article concluded:

> Unfortunately, great poetry is not enough in a world nurtured on sensation, novelty (often for novelty's sake) and grossly exaggerated public idolatry or disapproval. He was a talented actor and in order to 'put himself across' he played a part in public that the public has always relished, the hard drinking, booming, one-man cataclysm. Ultimately it killed him. The worthwhile memories of Dylan Thomas are tightly packed, totally condensed, in his own writings for everyone to read.

'Prologue' is a long poem and challenging to read aloud, but Aeron did so beautifully at the celebration of Fred's life at the Royal Society of Arts in London in 2000. She outlived Fred by only ten years, when she lost her battle with leukaemia. Aeron's ashes were interred by her family at the Boat House. Her last contact with Mary was at a small gathering for close family and friends in 2006 to mark Mary's passing.

Ceri's son-in-law Mel Gooding, a curator, writer and leading authority on twentieth-century British art, addressed the celebration at the Royal Society of Arts. In his obituary for *The Independent* he said of Fred's early work: 'The still life subjects of these extraordinary works are seen as through a crystalline glazed grid, a faceted transparent screen, behind which fish and fruit are transformed into mineral brilliancy. They are utterly unique in the art of their time.' The jazz musician George Melly had become a friend after opening a retrospective of Fred's work in 1988 at St David's Hall in Cardiff, Wales's national arts centre. He wrote in *The Guardian* that Fred seemed to be the personification of everything kind and decent. 'In contradiction to the words of the Bible,' Melly added, 'Janes was a prophet honoured in his own country. But he was certainly good enough to deserve much wider recognition.'

Fred with the musician George Melly at the opening of Fred's retrospective at St David's Hall, Cardiff in 1988

The Times' tribute was written by Alan Road, a distinguished Swansea-born journalist. As a neighbour in Dulwich, he got to know Fred well, and remarked that his sharp wit had not declined with old age. Fred's strict daily routine included at least one walk around Dulwich Park, which he loved, always following the same anti-clockwise route. Asked one year where he was going on holiday he replied: 'Round Dulwich Park in a clockwise direction'. An eccentric local who drove a go-kart led by huskies through the streets, forcing pedestrians to step aside, was dubbed 'Ben Cur', while the second wife of a friend who had married three times was known as 'the midwife'. Faced with a dilemma, Fred would decide to 'play it by deaf aid'.

As the millennium approached, the Glynn Vivian Art Gallery had asked Fred to mark it with a major retrospective of his work. When he died, Mel Gooding stepped in to curate it and, with his detached expert eye, chose the best examples of his sixty-year output, from his earliest still lifes of fruit from his father's shop, to the reworked paintings of the late 1980s and their suggestions of florist's flowers and Gower's cliffs and bays. The early portraits were there too – the first and last of Dylan; the images of Dan, Vernon and Tom Warner; three of Mervyn, charting a fifty-year relationship. In his catalogue essay Gooding wrote: 'The portraits of these brilliant Swansea friends … are those that will fix their image down all the years.'

Between them this small group of contemporaries contributed a huge amount not just to the cultural life of Wales but around the world in volumes of poetry, short stories, reference works on art, broadcasts and film scripts, orchestral and choral music, portraits and paintings rich and varied in both subject matter and stylistic approach. Their ability to teach and entertain while practising their craft and to embrace new media introduced younger generations to the beauty, stimulus and challenges they found themselves in the creative arts. The tragedy was that one of them paid such a high price for the fame his contribution brought.

4 March.
11

Pelican House
Laugharne.
Carms.

Dear Miss Ross.

Thanks so much
for your very kind invitation
for the "Tribute to Dylan"
at the Bishop's Gore School.
I'm very sorry but I shant be
able to come as I have been in
bed for a month, suffering from
Nervous Exhaustion & its now so
the Doctors tell me that the
troubles I had last year are
telling on me. I still cant believe
that I shant see my boy any
more, how I miss him I can
never tell, to think in one year
I lost my whole family, it's
been a very severe blow, one I'm
afraid I shall never really get
over.
Remember me to Fred & his
wife
        I am yours very
            Sincerely
                Florence. H. Thomas.

P. S. Caitlin is in London at the
moment so cant answer for
her, as I dont know when she
is returning.

APPENDIX I

Letter from Florence Thomas in 1954 to Ethel Ross about Dylan's death, from Dylan Thomas and the Amiateur Theatre *by Ethel Ross.*

Pelican House
Laugharne Carms.
11th March

Dear Miss Ross,

Thanks so much for your very kind invitation for the "tribute to Dylan" at the Bishop Gore School. I'm very sorry but I shan't be able to come as I have been in bed for a month, suffering from nervous exhaustion, + it's now so the Doctors tell me that the troubles I had last year are telling on me. I still can't believe that I shan't see my boy any more, how I miss him I can never tell, to think in one year I lost my whole family, it's been a very severe blow, one I'm afraid I shall never really get over. Remember me to Fred + his wife.

I am yours
    very Sincerely
        Florence H. Thomas

P.S. Caitlin is in London at the moment so can't answer for her, as I don't know when she is returning.

APPENDIX II

CWMRHYDYCEIRW ELEGIAC

Go, swallow, and tell, now that the summer is dying,
Spirits who loved him in time, where in the earth he is laid.
Dumb secrets are here, hard as the elm-roots in winter;
We who are left here confront words of inscrutable calm.
Life cuts into stone this that on earth is remembered,
How for the needs of the dead loving provision was made.
Strong words remain true, under the hammer of Babel:
Sleeps in the heart of the rock all that a god would restore.

Never shall time be stilled in the quarry of Cwmrhydyceirw,
Not while the boulder recoils under the force of the fuse.
Tablets imprisoned by rock, inert in the sleeping arena,
Quake in the shudder of air, knowing the swallow has passed.
One grief is enough, one tongue, to transfigure the ages:
Let our tears for the dead earn the forgiveness of dust.

Vernon Watkins
*A poem about the memorial stone Vernon Watkins
organised in 1963 for his friend Dylan Thomas*

PHOTO CREDITS

Part 1:

Dylan Thomas by Alfred Janes, 1934: National Museum of Wales ©
estate of Alfred Janes. *William Scott by Alfred Janes, 1933:* private
collection © estate of Alfred Janes. *Postcard from Dylan, 1934:* © Dylan
Thomas Estate. *Fred and Mervyn Levy washing up, c.1931:* © estate of
Alfred Janes. *Fred and Dylan sunbathing, c.1935:* courtesy of the William
Scott Foundation. Swansea Bay: © www.walesonview.com. *Charles
Fisher by Alfred Janes, 1937:* Jeff Towns/Dylan's Bookstore Collection
© estate of Alfred Janes. *Vernon Watkins by Alfred Janes, 1946:* courtesy
of the Watkins family © estate of Alfred Janes. *Fred in his Swansea
studio, c.1935:* © estate of Alfred Janes. *Caitlin Macnamara posing as a
dancer; Caitlin Macnamara lying by the river Avon, 1936:* © estate of Nora
Summers.

Part 2:

Dylan Thomas by Alfred Janes, 1953: Harry Ransom Centre, University
of Texas at Austin © estate of Alfred Janes. *Swansea Blitz, 1941:* ©
South Wales Evening Post. *Self-portrait in uniform by Alfred Janes, 1942:*
private collection © estate of Alfred Janes. *Mary Janes by Alfred Janes,
1942:* private collection © estate of Alfred Janes. *Tom Warner by Alfred
Janes, 1946:* private collection © estate of Alfred Janes. *Dylan Thomas
at the BBC:* photo by Francis Reiss/Picture Post/Getty Images. *Sketch
of Daniel Jones by Alfred Janes, 1947:* City & County of Swansea: Glynn
Vivian Art Gallery Collection © estate of Alfred Janes. *Dylan's
catalogue introduction, 1948:* courtesy of Desmond Morris © Dylan

251

Thomas Estate. *The Boat House in Laugharne:* photo by Terrence Spencer/Time Life Pictures/Getty Images. *Cover of the Radio Times, October 1949:* Dylan Thomas Centre Archive © Radio Times. *Dylan Thomas in New York, 1950:* photo by Hulton Archive/Getty Images. *Dylan and Pearl Kazin:* Jeff Towns/Dylan's Bookstore Collection. *A procession around Laugharne, 1948:* photo by Charles Hewitt/Picture Post/Getty Images. *Letter from Dylan Th omas to Alfred Janes, 1953:* © Dylan Thomas Estate. *Ceri Richards illustrations within Dylan Thomas's Collected Poems:* © estate of Ceri Richards. All rights reserved, DACS.

Part 3:
Dylan Thomas by Alfred Janes, 1964: City & County of Swansea: Glynn Vivian Art Gallery Collection © estate of Alfred Janes. *Florence Thomas, Fred and Hilly, c.1954:* © estate of Alfred Janes. *Fred Janes in his Gower studio, c.1960:* photo by Peter Johns. *Alfred Janes outside his home in Dulwich, 1966:* photo by Bernard Mitchell, courtesy National Library of Wales. *Caitlin, Aeronwy and Colm on their way to the High Court, 1966:* photo by Central Press/Getty Images. *Aeronwy Thomas Ellis, c.1976:* courtesy of Trefor Ellis. *In the garden at the Janeses' house, c.1971:* © estate of Alfred Janes. *Fred and Mervyn Levy washing up, c.1980s:* © Ross Janes. *Dylan Thomas's grave:* photo by Kevin Cummins/Getty Images. *Fred and George Melly, 1988:* © Hilly Janes. *Hannah Ellis:* © South Wales Evening Post.

Appendices:
Letter from Florence Thomas to Ethel Ross, 1954: estate of Ethel Ross. *Cwmrhydyceirw Elegiac by Vernon Watkins:* courtesy of Gwen Watkins © estate of Vernon Watkins.

ACKNOWLEDGEMENTS

My aim has been to tell Dylan's story through his voice and in the words of those closest to him. Books by the following authors have therefore been vital resources: John Malcolm Brinnin, *Dylan Thomas in America*; Daniel Jones, *My Friend Dylan Thomas*; Caitlin Thomas with George Tremlett, *Caitlin: A Warring Absence*; Aeronwy Thomas, *My Father's Places*; Gwen Watkins, *Portrait of a Friend* and *Cracking the Luftwaffe Codes*.

In addition to these, I have found Andrew Lycett's *Dylan Thomas: A New Life* to be the most scholarly biography on which to rely for factual information and to fill in the gaps. Also valuable have been Heather Holt's *Dylan Thomas the Actor*; David N. Thomas's two volumes of edited transcripts of interviews by Colin Edwards and Constantine Fitzgibbon, *Dylan Remembered Volumes 1 and 2*; *The Life of Dylan Thomas* by Constantine Fitzgibbon; *Dylan Thomas, the Collected Letters*, edited by Paul Ferris, and his biography *Caitlin*; and archive material from the Dylan Thomas Society (thedylanthomassocietyofgb.co.uk). Dylan's agents, David Higham Associates, have been very kind in allowing me to reproduce so much of his writing. I have used the following editions: *Collected Poems 1934-1953*, 2000; *Collected Stories*, 2003; *Under Milk Wood*, Definitive Edition, 2000, all by Orion Books; and *Miscellany*, 1963, Dent & Sons for the BBC broadcasts *Return Journey* and *Reminiscences of Childhood*.

I am very grateful to all the people closely associated with Dylan and his friends who granted me interviews and/or provided me with source material, especially Hannah Ellis, his granddaughter, and Trefor Ellis, his son-in-law; also Glenys Cour, Valerie Dawson, Professor John Goodby, Mel and Rhiannon Gooding, Andrew Gordon of David Higham Associates, Fiona Green, Bruce Hunter, Ceri Levy, Desmond Morris, Cathy and Rob Roberts, Michael Rush of the Dylan Thomas Trust, Jeff Towns and Gwen Watkins and her family who kindly also gave permission to reproduce work by Vernon Watkins.

I am also grateful for access to interviews with my late father by Professor Tony Curtis in *Planet* magazine and *Welsh Artists Talking*, and by Dr Ceri Thomas in *Cambria* magazine.

Other sources include the BBC, the *Daily Telegraph*, *The Guardian*, *The Independent*, poemhunter.com, The Poetry Foundation, *South Wales Evening Post*, West Glamorgan Archive (and Dr David Morris in particular), *Texas Quarterly*, *The Times* and yorku.ca/caitlin/kardomah (for Charles Fisher).

My thanks are due to Graham Matthews for use of his excellent photographs of my father's work, and also to the staff of the Glynn Vivian Art Gallery, National Museum and Art Gallery of Wales, National Library of Wales, the Dylan Thomas Centre, Bernard Mitchell, Gabriel and Leonie Summers for their co-operation in sourcing images. Kirstin Sinclair took the photograph of me on the jacket.

No modern biographer can go without thanking all the creators and users of digital platforms and social media, often strangers, but who lead to new information, resources and news. Andrew Dally of @DylanThomasNews is essential reading in this respect (how wonderful Dylan Thomas would have been on Twitter). And finally, for their encouragement, patience and professionalism, heartfelt thanks to everyone at Parthian Books; and to my family and friends – Andrew, Alex and Suzi Pozniak, Ross Janes, Cat Brown, Professor Anne Murcott and Susan Aldworth.

Hilly Janes